W0265828

The Importance of Being Earnest

A Trivial Comedy for Serious People

edited by
Harold Fish

Cornelsen

The Importance of Being Earnest

Herausgegeben von
Harold Fish

Verlagsredaktion
Neil Porter

Technische Umsetzung
Ingo Ostermaier

Umschlagillustrationen
Großes Bild: © Getty Images/Eileen Darby,
kleines Bild: Getty Images/Thurston Hopkins

Herausgeber der *Cornelsen Senior English Library:*
Prof. Dr. Albert-Reiner Glaap

www.cornelsen.de

1. Auflage, 3. Druck 2009

Alle Drucke dieser Auflage sind inhaltlich unverändert und können
im Unterricht nebeneinander verwendet werden.

© 2005 Cornelsen Verlag, Berlin

Das Werk und seine Teile sind urheberrechtlich geschützt.
Jede Nutzung in anderen als den gesetzlich zugelassenen Fällen bedarf der
vorherigen schriftlichen Einwilligung des Verlages.
Hinweis zu den §§46, 52a UrhG: Weder das Werk noch seine Teile dürfen
ohne eine solche Einwilligung eingescannt und in ein Netzwerk eingestellt
oder sonst öffentlich zugänglich gemacht werden. Dies gilt auch für
Intranets von Schulen und sonstigen Bildungseinrichtungen.

Druck: CS-Druck CornelsenStürtz, Berlin

ISBN 978-3-464-31057-1

Inhalt gedruckt auf säurefreiem Papier aus nachhaltiger Forstwirtschaft.

Contents

To

ROBERT BALDWIN ROSS

In Appreciation
and
Affection

Abbreviations and Annotations

abbr	abbreviation	n	noun
adj	adjective	p., pp.	page, pages
cf.	confer; see	pl	plural
derog	derogatory	sb.	somebody
e.g.	exempli gratia; for example	sing	singular
esp.	especially	sl	slang
etc.	et cetera; and so on	sth.	something
fml	formal	usu.	usually
infml	informal	v	verb
jdm./jdn.	jemandem/en		

The annotations are arranged chronologically: the first time a word is used in a story is where you will find it explained.

The Persons in the Play

JOHN WORTHING, J.P.
ALGERNON MONCRIEFF
REV. CANON CHASUBLE, D.D.
MERRIMAN, *Butler*
LANE, *Manservant*
LADY BRACKNELL
HON. GWENDOLEN FAIRFAX
CECILY CARDEW
MISS PRISM, *Governess*

The Scenes of the Play

ACT I
Algernon Moncrieff's flat in Half-Moon Street, W.

ACT II
The garden at the Manor House, Woolton.

ACT III
Drawing-room at the Manor House, Woolton.

TIME
The Present.

▷ *Worthing* ['wɜːðɪŋ] • *J.P.* (abbr) = *Justice of the Peace:* judge who is often untrained but is allowed to make judgements on minor legal matters • *Algernon* ['ældʒənən] • *Moncrieff* [mən'kriːf] • *Rev.* (abbr) = *Reverend:* title of a clergyman in the Protestant church • *Chasuble* ['tʃæzjʊbəl] • *D.D.* (abbr): Doctor of Divinity • *Hon.* (abbr) = *Honourable:* title given to sons and daughters of certain aristocrats • *W.*: West London

FIRST ACT

Scene: Morning-room in Algernon's flat in Half-Moon Street. The room is luxuriously and artistically furnished. The sound of a piano is heard in the adjoining room.
LANE *is arranging afternoon tea on the table and, after the music has ceased,* ALGERNON *enters.*

ALGERNON: Did you hear what I was playing, Lane?

LANE: I didn't think it polite to listen, sir.

ALGERNON: I'm sorry for that, for your sake. I don't play accurately – anyone can play accurately – but I play with wonderful expression. As far as the piano is concerned, sentiment is my forte. I keep science for Life.

LANE: Yes, sir.

ALGERNON: And, speaking of the science of Life, have you got the cucumber sandwiches cut for Lady Bracknell?

LANE: Yes, sir. [*Hands them on a salver.*]

ALGERNON: [*Inspects them, takes two, and sits down on the sofa.*] Oh! ... by the way, Lane, I see from your book that on Thursday night, when Lord Shoreham and Mr Worthing were dining with me, eight bottles of champagne are entered as having been consumed.

LANE: Yes, sir; eight bottles and a pint.

ALGERNON: Why is it that at a bachelor's establishment the servants invariably drink the champagne? I ask merely for information.

▷ **10** *sentiment:* emotion, feelings • *forte* ['fɔːteɪ]: strength **15** *salver:* tray (usu. made of silver) on which servants hand cards, letters etc. **19** *enter sth.:* record sth. (in a book of lists of things eaten in a household) **21** *pint* [paɪnt]: ca. 0.5 litres **22** *establishment:* (here) home **23** *invariably:* always • *merely:* (here) only

LANE: I attribute it to the superior quality of the wine, sir. I have often observed that in married households the champagne is rarely of a first-rate brand.

ALGERNON: Good heavens! Is marriage so demoralizing as that?

LANE: I believe it *is* a very pleasant state, sir. I have had very little experience of it myself up to the present. I have only been married once. That was in consequence of a misunderstanding between myself and a young person.

ALGERNON: [*Languidly.*] I don't know that I am much interested in your family life, Lane.

LANE: No, sir; it is not a very interesting subject. I never think of it myself.

ALGERNON: Very natural, I am sure. That will do, Lane, thank you.

LANE: Thank you, sir.

[LANE *goes out.*]

ALGERNON: Lane's views on marriage seem somewhat lax. Really, if the lower orders don't set us a good example, what on earth is the use of them? They seem, as a class, to have absolutely no sense of moral responsibility.

[*Enter* LANE.]

LANE: Mr Ernest Worthing.

[*Enter* JACK. LANE *goes out.*]

ALGERNON: How are you, my dear Ernest? What brings you up to town?

JACK: Oh, pleasure, pleasure! What else should bring one anywhere? Eating as usual, I see, Algy!

ALGERNON: [*Stiffly.*] I believe it is customary in good society to take some slight refreshment at five o'clock. Where have you been since last Thursday?

JACK: [*Sitting down on the sofa.*] In the country.

ALGERNON: What on earth do you do there?

JACK: [*Pulling off his gloves.*] When one is in town one amuses oneself. When one is in the country one amuses other people. It is excessively boring.

ALGERNON: And who are the people you amuse?

JACK: [*Airily.*] Oh, neighbours, neighbours.

ALGERNON: Got nice neighbours in your part of Shropshire?

JACK: Perfectly horrid! Never speak to one of them.

ALGERNON: How immensely you must amuse them! [*Goes over and takes sandwich.*] By the way, Shropshire is your county, is it not?

JACK: Eh? Shropshire? Yes, of course. Hallo! Why all these cups? Why cucumber sandwiches? Why such reckless extravagance in one so young? Who is coming to tea?

ALGERNON: Oh! merely Aunt Augusta and Gwendolen.

JACK: How perfectly delightful!

ALGERNON: Yes, that is all very well; but I am afraid Aunt Augusta won't quite approve of your being here.

JACK: May I ask why?

ALGERNON: My dear fellow, the way you flirt with Gwendolen is perfectly disgraceful. It is almost as bad as the way Gwendolen flirts with you.

▷ **1** *attribute sth. to sth. else:* consider sth. to be the result of sth. else **9** *languid:* lässig, träge **16** *lax:* not morally strict or careful **17** *lower orders* (pl): lower social classes **27** *customary:* usual, normal **36** *airily:* in a casual tone **37** *Shropshire:* English county on the border with Wales **42** *reckless extravagance:* irresponsible wastefulness **47** *approve of sth.:* think that sth. is good **50** *perfectly disgraceful:* totally unacceptable

JACK: I am in love with Gwendolen. I have come up to town expressly to propose to her.

ALGERNON: I thought you had come up for pleasure? ... I call that business.

JACK: How utterly unromantic you are!

ALGERNON: I really don't see anything romantic in proposing. It is very romantic to be in love. But there is nothing romantic about a definite proposal. Why, one may be accepted. One usually is, I believe. Then the excitement is all over. The very essence of romance is uncertainty. If ever I get married, I'll certainly try to forget the fact.

JACK: I have no doubt about that, dear Algy. The Divorce Court was specially invented for people whose memories are so curiously constituted.

ALGERNON: Oh! there is no use speculating on that subject. Divorces are made in Heaven – [JACK *puts out his hand to take a sandwich.* ALGERNON *at once interferes.*] Please don't touch the cucumber sandwiches. They are ordered specially for Aunt Augusta. [*Takes one and eats it.*]

JACK: Well, you have been eating them all the time.

ALGERNON: That is quite a different matter. She is my aunt. [*Takes plate from below.*] Have some bread and butter. The bread and butter is for Gwendolen. Gwendolen is devoted to bread and butter.

JACK: [*Advancing to table and helping himself.*] And very good bread and butter it is too.

ALGERNON: Well, my dear fellow, you need not eat as if you were going to eat it all. You behave as if you were married to her already. You are not married to her already, and I don't think you ever will be.

JACK: Why on earth do you say that?

ALGERNON: Well, in the first place, girls never marry the men they flirt with. Girls don't think it right.

JACK: Oh, that is nonsense!

ALGERNON: It isn't. It is a great truth. It accounts for the extraordinary number of bachelors that one sees all over the place. In the second place, I don't give my consent.

JACK: Your consent!

ALGERNON: My dear fellow, Gwendolen is my first cousin. And before I allow you to marry her, you will have to clear up the whole question of Cecily. [*Rings bell.*]

JACK: Cecily! What on earth do you mean? What do you mean, Algy, by Cecily! I don't know any one of the name of Cecily.

[*Enter* LANE.]

ALGERNON: Bring me that cigarette case Mr Worthing left in the smoking-room the last time he dined here.

LANE: Yes, sir.

[LANE *goes out.*]

JACK: Do you mean to say you have had my cigarette case all this time? I wish to goodness you had let me know. I have been writing frantic letters to Scotland Yard about it. I was very nearly offering a large reward.

ALGERNON: Well, I wish you would offer one. I happen to be more than usually hard up.

JACK: There is no good offering a large reward now that the thing is found.

▷ **1** *expressly:* for a special purpose **2** *propose to sb.:* ask sb. to marry you **14** *constituted:* made in a particular way **34** *account for sth.:* be the reason for sth. **36** *consent* (n): permission **39** *clear sth. up:* explain sth. **49** *to goodness:* used to emphasize sth. **52–53** *be hard up:* have little money

[Enter LANE *with the cigarette case on a salver. Algernon takes it at once.* LANE *goes out.]*

ALGERNON: I think that is rather mean of you, Ernest, I must say. [*Opens case and examines it.*] However, it makes no matter, for, now that I look at the inscription inside, I find that the thing isn't yours after all.

JACK: Of course it's mine. [*Moving to him.*] You have seen me with it a hundred times, and you have no right whatsoever to read what is written inside. It is a very ungentlemanly thing to read a private cigarette case.

ALGERNON: Oh! it is absurd to have a hard and fast rule about what one should read and what one shouldn't. More than half of modern culture depends on what one shouldn't read.

JACK: I am quite aware of the fact, and I don't propose to discuss modern culture. It isn't the sort of thing one should talk of in private. I simply want my cigarette case back.

ALGERNON: Yes; but this isn't your cigarette case. This cigarette case is a present from someone of the name of Cecily, and you said you didn't know anyone of that name.

JACK: Well, if you want to know, Cecily happens to be my aunt.

ALGERNON: Your aunt!

JACK: Yes. Charming old lady she is, too. Lives at Tunbridge Wells. Just give it back to me, Algy.

ALGERNON: [*Retreating to back of sofa.*] But why does she call herself little Cecily if she is your aunt and lives at Tunbridge Wells? [*Reading.*] 'From little Cecily with her fondest love.'

JACK: [*Moving to sofa and kneeling upon it.*] My dear fellow, what on earth is there in that? Some aunts are tall, some aunts are not tall. That is a matter that surely an aunt may be allowed to decide for herself. You seem to think that every aunt should be exactly like your aunt! That is absurd! For Heaven's sake give me back my cigarette case. [*Follows* ALGERNON *round the room.*]

ALGERNON: Yes. But why does your aunt call you her uncle? 'From little Cecily, with her fondest love to her dear Uncle Jack.' There is no objection, I admit, to an aunt being a small aunt, but why an aunt, no matter what her size may be, should call her own nephew her uncle, I can't quite make out. Besides, your name isn't Jack at all; it is Ernest.

JACK: It isn't Ernest; it's Jack.

ALGERNON: You have always told me it was Ernest. I have introduced you to everyone as Ernest. You answer to the name of Ernest. You look as if your name was Ernest. You are the most earnest-looking person I ever saw in my life. It is perfectly absurd your saying that your name isn't Ernest. It's on your cards. Here is one of them. [*Taking it from case.*] 'Mr Ernest Worthing, B.4, The Albany.' I'll keep this as a proof that your name is Ernest if ever you attempt to deny it to me, or to Gwendolen, or to anyone else. [*Puts the card in his pocket.*]

JACK: Well, my name is Ernest in town and Jack in the country, and the cigarette case was given to me in the country.

ALGERNON: Yes, but that does not account for the fact that your small Aunt Cecily, who lives at Tunbridge Wells, calls you her dear uncle. Come, old boy, you had much better have the thing out at once.

JACK: My dear Algy, you talk exactly as if you were a dentist. It is very vulgar to talk like a dentist when one isn't a dentist. It produces a false impression.

ALGERNON: Well, that is exactly what dentists always do. Now, go on! Tell me the whole thing. I may mention that I have always suspected you of being a confirmed and secret Bunburyist; and I am quite sure of it now.

▷ **3** *mean* (adj): not generous **14** *propose:* intend **22** *Tunbridge Wells:* a formerly fashionable spa town south-east of London **26** *fond:* affectionate **31** *for Heaven's sake:* um Himmels willen **45** *The Albany:* bachelor flats in central London **47** *deny sth. to sb.:* say to sb. that sth. is untrue **53** *have the thing out:* explain the situation **59** *confirmed:* überzeugte(r), eingefleischte(r)

JACK: Bunburyist? What on earth do you mean by a Bunburyist?

ALGERNON: I'll reveal to you the meaning of that incomparable expression as soon as you are kind enough to inform me why you are Ernest in town and Jack in the country.

JACK: Well, produce my cigarette case first.

ALGERNON: Here it is. [*Hands cigarette case.*] Now produce your explanation, and pray make it improbable. [*Sits on sofa.*]

JACK: My dear fellow, there is nothing improbable about my explanation at all. In fact it's perfectly ordinary. Old Mr Thomas Cardew, who adopted me when I was a little boy, made me in his will guardian to his granddaughter, Miss Cecily Cardew. Cecily, who addresses me as her uncle from motives of respect that you could not possibly appreciate, lives at my place in the country under the charge of her admirable governess, Miss Prism.

ALGERNON: Where is that place in the country, by the way?

JACK: That is nothing to you, dear boy. You are not going to be invited … I may tell you candidly that the place is not in Shropshire.

ALGERNON: I suspected that, my dear fellow! I have Bunburyed all over Shropshire on two separate occasions. Now, go on. Why are you Ernest in town and Jack in the country?

JACK: My dear Algy, I don't know whether you will be able to understand my real motives. You are hardly serious enough. When one is placed in the position of guardian, one has to adopt a very high moral tone on all subjects. It's one's duty to do so. And as a high moral tone can hardly be said to conduce very much to either one's health or one's happiness, in order to get up to town I have always pretended to have a younger brother of the name of Ernest, who lives in the Albany, and gets into the most dreadful scrapes. That, my dear Algy, is the whole truth pure and simple.

ALGERNON: The truth is rarely pure and never simple. Modern life would be very tedious if it were either, and modern literature a complete impossibility!

JACK: That wouldn't be at all a bad thing.

ALGERNON: Literary criticism is not your forte, my dear fellow. Don't try it. You should leave that to people who haven't been at a University. They do it so well in the daily papers. What you really are is a Bunburyist. I was quite right in saying you were a Bunburyist. You are one of the most advanced Bunburyists I know.

JACK: What on earth do you mean?

ALGERNON: You have invented a very useful younger brother called Ernest, in order that you may be able to come up to town as often as you like. I have invented an invaluable permanent invalid called Bunbury, in order that I may be able to go down into the country whenever I choose. Bunbury is perfectly invaluable. If it wasn't for Bunbury's extraordinary bad health, for instance, I wouldn't be able to dine with you at Willis's tonight, for I have been really engaged to Aunt Augusta for more than a week.

JACK: I haven't asked you to dine with me anywhere tonight.

ALGERNON: I know. You are absurdly careless about sending out invitations. It is very foolish of you. Nothing annoys people so much as not receiving invitations.

JACK: You had much better dine with your Aunt Augusta.

▷ **2** *reveal sth.:* explain sth. that is not understood • *incomparable* [ɪn'kɒmprəbl]: that cannot be compared with anything else **5** *produce sth.:* (here) hand sth. over **7** *pray* (fml): please • *improbable:* hard to believe **10** *will* (n): Testament **11** *guardian:* Vormund **13** *appreciate sth.* [ə'pri:ʃieɪt]: understand the good qualities of sth. **14** *admirable:* excellent **17** *candid:* honest, direct **19** *suspect sth.* [-'-]: have the feeling that sth. is true **26** *conduce to sth.:* improve sth. **29** *dreadful:* terrible • *scrape* (n): unpleasant or difficult situation **32** *tedious* ['ti:diəs]: boring **44** *invaluable:* extremely useful • *invalid* ['ɪnvəlɪd] (n): very sick person **48** *Willis's* ['wɪlɪsɪz]: fashionable London restaurant in the 1890s **48–49** *be engaged to sb.:* (here) have an appointment with sb.

ALGERNON: I haven't the smallest intention of doing anything of the kind. To begin with, I dined there on Monday, and once a week is quite enough to dine with one's own relations. In the second place, whenever I do dine there I am always treated as a member of the family, and sent down with either no woman at all, or two. In the third place, I know perfectly well whom she will place me next to, tonight. She will place me next Mary Farquhar, who always flirts with her own husband across the dinner-table. That is not very pleasant. Indeed, it is not even decent ... and that sort of thing is enormously on the increase. The amount of women in London who flirt with their own husbands is perfectly scandalous. It looks so bad. It is simply washing one's clean linen in public. Besides, now that I know you to be a confirmed Bunburyist I naturally want to talk to you about Bunburying. I want to tell you the rules.

JACK: I'm not a Bunburyist at all. If Gwendolen accepts me, I am going to kill my brother, indeed I think I'll kill him in any case. Cecily is a little too much interested in him. It is rather a bore. So I am going to get rid of Ernest. And I strongly advise you to do the same with Mr ... with your invalid friend who has the absurd name.

ALGERNON: Nothing will induce me to part with Bunbury, and if you ever get married, which seems to me extremely problematic, you will be very glad to know Bunbury. A man who marries without knowing Bunbury has a very tedious time of it.

JACK: That is nonsense. If I marry a charming girl like Gwendolen, and she is the only girl I ever saw in my life that I would marry, I certainly won't want to know Bunbury.

ALGERNON: Then your wife will. You don't seem to realize, that in married life three is company and two is none.

JACK: [*Sententiously.*] That, my dear young friend, is the theory that the corrupt French Drama has been propounding for the last fifty years.

ALGERNON: Yes; and that the happy English home has proved in half the time.

JACK: For heaven's sake, don't try to be cynical. It's perfectly easy to be cynical.

ALGERNON: My dear fellow, it isn't easy to be anything nowadays. There's such a lot of beastly competition about. [*The sound of an electric bell is heard.*] Ah! that must be Aunt Augusta. Only relatives, or creditors, ever ring in that Wagnerian manner. Now, if I get her out of the way for ten minutes, so that you can have an opportunity for proposing to Gwendolen, may I dine with you tonight at Willis's?

JACK: I suppose so, if you want to.

ALGERNON: Yes, but you must be serious about it. I hate people who are not serious about meals. It is so shallow of them.

[*Enter* LANE.]

LANE: Lady Bracknell and Miss Fairfax.

[ALGERNON *goes forward to meet them. Enter* LADY BRACKNELL *and* GWENDOLEN.]

LADY BRACKNELL: Good afternoon, dear Algernon, I hope you are behaving very well.

ALGERNON: I'm feeling very well, Aunt Augusta.

LADY BRACKNELL: That's not quite the same thing. In fact the two things rarely go together. [*Sees* JACK *and bows to him with icy coldness.*]

ALGERNON: [*To* GWENDOLEN.] Dear me, you are smart!

GWENDOLEN: I am always smart! Aren't I, Mr Worthing?

▷ **1–2** *(nothing) of the kind:* used to emphasize the opposite of what has been said **5** *send sb. down with sb. else:* (here) arrange for sb. to accompany sb. else of the opposite sex into the dining room and to sit next to them at dinner **9** *decent* ['di:sənt] (adj): proper, well mannered **17** *rather a bore:* (here) inconvenient **20** *induce sb. to do sth.:* persuade sb. to do sth. **29** *sententious:* trying to sound important and intelligent but actually sounding pompous **30** *propound sth.:* put sth. (e.g. an idea or theory) forward **39** *Wagnerian manner:* (here) loudly and persistently

JACK: You're quite perfect, Miss Fairfax.

GWENDOLEN: Oh! I hope I am not that. It would leave no room for developments, and I intend to develop in many directions. [GWENDOLEN *and* JACK *sit down together in the corner.*]

LADY BRACKNELL: I'm sorry if we are a little late, Algernon, but I was obliged to call on dear Lady Harbury. I hadn't been there since her poor husband's death. I never saw a woman so altered; she looks quite twenty years younger. And now I'll have a cup of tea, and one of those nice cucumber sandwiches you promised me.

ALGERNON: Certainly, Aunt Augusta. [*Goes over to tea-table.*]

LADY BRACKNELL: Won't you come and sit here, Gwendolen?

GWENDOLEN: Thanks, mamma, I'm quite comfortable where I am.

ALGERNON: [*Picking up empty plate in horror.*] Good heavens! Lane! Why are there no cucumber sandwiches? I ordered them specially.

LANE: [*Gravely.*] There were no cucumbers in the market this morning, sir. I went down twice.

ALGERNON: No cucumbers!

LANE: No, sir. Not even for ready money.

ALGERNON: That will do, Lane, thank you.

LANE: Thank you, sir. [*Goes out.*]

ALGERNON: I am greatly distressed, Aunt Augusta, about there being no cucumbers, not even for ready money.

LADY BRACKNELL: It really makes no matter, Algernon. I had some crumpets with Lady Harbury, who seems to me to be living entirely for pleasure now.

ALGERNON: I hear her hair has turned quite gold from grief.

LADY BRACKNELL: It certainly has changed its colour. From what cause I, of course, cannot say. [ALGERNON *crosses and hands tea.*]

Thank you. I've quite a treat for you tonight, Algernon. I am going to send you down with Mary Farquhar. She is such a nice woman, and so attentive to her husband. It's delightful to watch them.

ALGERNON: I am afraid, Aunt Augusta, I shall have to give up the pleasure of dining with you tonight after all.

LADY BRACKNELL: [*Frowning.*] I hope not, Algernon. It would put my table completely out. Your uncle would have to dine upstairs. Fortunately he is accustomed to that.

ALGERNON: It is a great bore, and, I need hardly say, a terrible disappointment to me, but the fact is I have just had a telegram to say that my poor friend Bunbury is very ill again. [*Exchanges glances with* JACK.] They seem to think I should be with him.

LADY BRACKNELL: It is very strange. This Mr Bunbury seems to suffer from curiously bad health.

ALGERNON: Yes; poor Bunbury is a dreadful invalid.

LADY BRACKNELL: Well, I must say, Algernon, that I think it is high time that Mr Bunbury made up his mind whether he was going to live or to die. This shilly-shallying with the question is absurd. Nor do I in any way approve of the modern sympathy with invalids. I consider it morbid. Illness of any kind is hardly a thing to be encouraged in others. Health is the primary duty of life. I am always telling that to your poor uncle, but he never seems to take much notice ... as far as any improvement in his ailment goes. I should be much obliged if you would ask Mr Bunbury, from me, to be kind enough not to have a relapse on Saturday, for I rely on you to arrange my music for me. It is my last reception, and one wants

▷ **6** *call on sb.:* make a social visit to sb. **7** *altered* (adj): changed **16** *grave* (adj): serious **22** *greatly distressed:* extremely sorry **25** *crumpet:* soft cake made with yeast (= Hefe) and baked on an iron plate **27** *grief:* sadness **32** *be attentive to sb.:* take care of sb.'s needs **35** *frown* [fraʊn]: die Stirn runzeln **35–36** *it would put my table completely out:* das brächte meine Tischordnung vollständig durcheinander **47** *shilly-shallying* (n): inability to decide on sth. **49** *morbid:* having a strong interest in unpleasant matters (e.g. illness and death) **52** *ailment* ['eɪlmənt]: illness **54** *have a relapse:* fall sick again

something that will encourage conversation, particularly at the end of the season when everyone has practically said whatever they had to say, which, in most cases, was probably not much.

Algernon: I'll speak to Bunbury, Aunt Augusta, if he is still conscious, and I think I can promise you he'll be all right by Saturday. Of course the music is a great difficulty. You see, if one plays good music, people don't listen, and if one plays bad music people don't talk. But I'll run over the programme I've drawn out, if you will kindly come into the next room for a moment.

Lady Bracknell: Thank you, Algernon. It is very thoughtful of you. [*Rising, and following* Algernon.] I'm sure the programme will be delightful, after a few expurgations. French songs I cannot possibly allow. People always seem to think that they are improper, and either look shocked, which is vulgar, or laugh, which is worse. But German sounds a thoroughly respectable language, and indeed, I believe is so. Gwendolen, you will accompany me.

Gwendolen: Certainly, mamma.

[Lady Bracknell *and* Algernon *go into the music-room,* Gwendolen *remains behind.*]

Jack: Charming day it has been, Miss Fairfax.

Gwendolen: Pray don't talk to me about the weather, Mr Worthing. Whenever people talk to me about the weather, I always feel quite certain that they mean something else. And that makes me so nervous.

Jack: I do mean something else.

Gwendolen: I thought so. In fact, I am never wrong.

Jack: And I would like to be allowed to take advantage of Lady Bracknell's temporary absence …

Gwendolen: I would certainly advise you to do so. Mamma has a way of coming back suddenly into a room that I have often had to speak to her about.

JACK: [*Nervously.*] Miss Fairfax, ever since I met you I have admired you more than any girl ... I have ever met since ... I met you.

GWENDOLEN: Yes, I am quite well aware of the fact. And I often wish that in public, at any rate, you had been more demonstrative. For me you have always had an irresistible fascination. Even before I met you I was far from indifferent to you. [JACK *looks at her in amazement.*] We live, as I hope you know, Mr Worthing, in an age of ideals. The fact is constantly mentioned in the more expensive monthly magazines, and has reached the provincial pulpits, I am told; and my ideal has always been to love someone of the name of Ernest. There is something in that name that inspires absolute confidence. The moment Algernon first mentioned to me that he had a friend called Ernest, I knew I was destined to love you.

JACK: You really love me, Gwendolen?

GWENDOLEN: Passionately!

JACK: Darling! You don't know how happy you've made me.

GWENDOLEN: My own Ernest!

JACK: But you don't really mean to say that you couldn't love me if my name wasn't Ernest?

GWENDOLEN: But your name is Ernest.

JACK: Yes, I know it is. But supposing it was something else? Do you mean to say you couldn't love me then?

GWENDOLEN: [*Glibly.*] Ah! that is clearly a metaphysical speculation, and like most metaphysical speculations has very little reference at all to the actual facts of real life, as we know them.

JACK: Personally, darling, to speak quite candidly, I don't much care about the name of Ernest ... I don't think the name suits me at all.

▷ **2** *season:* winter period when the upper-classes live in London **8** *run over sth.:* check sth. **12** *a few expurgations* [ˌekspəˈgeɪʃən]: the removal of a few items **35** *demonstrative* [- ˈ- - -]: show feelings of love openly **40** *provincial pulpits:* (here) churches outside London **54** *glib:* (here) trying to be too clever

GWENDOLEN: It suits you perfectly. It is a divine name. It has a music of its own. It produces vibrations.

JACK: Well, really, Gwendolen, I must say that I think there are lots of other much nicer names. I think Jack, for instance, a charming name.

GWENDOLEN: Jack? ... No, there is very little music in the name Jack, if any at all, indeed. It does not thrill. It produces absolutely no vibrations ... I have known several Jacks, and they all, without exception, were more than usually plain. Besides, Jack is a notorious domesticity for John! And I pity any woman who is married to a man called John. She would probably never be allowed to know the entrancing pleasure of a single moment's solitude. The only really safe name is Ernest.

JACK: Gwendolen, I must get christened at once – I mean we must get married at once. There is no time to be lost.

GWENDOLEN: Married, Mr Worthing?

JACK: [*Astounded.*] Well ... surely. You know that I love you, and you led me to believe, Miss Fairfax, that you were not absolutely indifferent to me.

GWENDOLEN: I adore you. But you haven't proposed to me yet. Nothing has been said at all about marriage. The subject has not even been touched on.

JACK: Well ... may I propose to you now?

GWENDOLEN: I think it would be an admirable opportunity. And to spare you any possible disappointment, Mr Worthing, I think it only fair to tell you quite frankly beforehand that I am fully determined to accept you.

JACK: Gwendolen!

GWENDOLEN: Yes, Mr Worthing, what have you got to say to me?

JACK: You know what I have got to say to you.

GWENDOLEN: Yes, but you don't say it.

JACK: Gwendolen, will you marry me? [*Goes on his knees.*]

GWENDOLEN: Of course I will, darling. How long you have been about it! I am afraid you have had very little experience in how to propose.

JACK: My own one, I have never loved anyone in the world but you.

GWENDOLEN: Yes, but men often propose for practice. I know my brother Gerald does. All my girl-friends tell me so. What wonderfully blue eyes you have, Ernest! They are quite, quite, blue. I hope you will always look at me just like that, especially when there are other people present. [*Enter* LADY BRACKNELL.]

LADY BRACKNELL: Mr Worthing! Rise, sir, from this semi-recumbent posture. It is most indecorous.

GWENDOLEN: Mamma! [*He tries to rise; she restrains him.*] I must beg you to retire. This is no place for you. Besides, Mr Worthing has not quite finished yet.

LADY BRACKNELL: Finished what, may I ask?

GWENDOLEN: I am engaged to Mr Worthing, mamma. [*They rise together.*]

LADY BRACKNELL: Pardon me, you are not engaged to anyone. When you do become engaged to someone, I, or your father, should his health permit him, will inform you of the fact. An engagement should come on a young girl as a surprise, pleasant or unpleasant, as the case may be. It is hardly a matter that she could be allowed to arrange for herself ... And now I have a few questions to put to you, Mr Worthing. While I am making these inquiries, you, Gwendolen, will wait for me below in the carriage.

▷ **9** *plain* (adj): unattractive **10** *notorious:* well-known for being unpleasant • *domesticity:* (here) intimate family name **12** *entrancing pleasure:* pleasure that fills sb. with joy **13** *solitude* (n): state of being alone **14** *get christened:* sich taufen lassen **19** *indifferent to sb./sth.:* having no feelings for sb./sth. **42–43** *semi-recumbent posture:* position in which sb. is half lying **43** *indecorous:* ugly, showing bad manners **44** *restrain sb.:* hold sb. down or back **45** *retire:* go into another room

Gwendolen: [*Reproachfully.*] Mamma!

Lady Bracknell: In the carriage, Gwendolen! [Gwendolen *goes to the door. She and* Jack *blow kisses to each other behind* Lady Bracknell*'s back.* Lady Bracknell *looks vaguely about as if she could not understand what the noise was. Finally turns round.*] Gwendolen, the carriage!

Gwendolen: Yes, mamma. [*Goes out, looking back at* Jack.]

Lady Bracknell: [*Sitting down.*] You can take a seat, Mr Worthing.

[*Looks in her pocket for note-book and pencil.*]

Jack: Thank you, Lady Bracknell, I prefer standing.

Lady Bracknell: [*Pencil and note-book in hand.*] I feel bound to tell you that you are not down on my list of eligible young men, although I have the same list as the dear Duchess of Bolton has. We work together, in fact. However, I am quite ready to enter your name, should your answers be what a really affectionate mother requires. Do you smoke?

Jack: Well, yes, I must admit I smoke.

Lady Bracknell: I am glad to hear it. A man should always have an occupation of some kind. There are far too many idle men in London as it is. How old are you?

Jack: Twenty-nine.

Lady Bracknell: A very good age to be married at. I have always been of opinion that a man who desires to get married should know either everything or nothing. Which do you know?

Jack: [*After some hesitation.*] I know nothing, Lady Bracknell.

Lady Bracknell: I am pleased to hear it. I do not approve of anything that tampers with natural ignorance. Ignorance is like a delicate exotic fruit; touch it and the bloom is gone. The whole theory of modern education is radically unsound. Fortunately in England, at any rate, education produces no effect whatsoever. If it did, it would prove a serious danger to the upper classes, and probably lead to acts of violence in Grosvenor Square. What is your income?

JACK: Between seven and eight thousand a year.

LADY BRACKNELL: [*Makes a note in her book.*] In land, or in investments?

JACK: In investments, chiefly.

LADY BRACKNELL: That is satisfactory. What between the duties expected of one during one's lifetime, and the duties exacted from one after one's death, land has ceased to be either a profit or a pleasure. It gives one position, and prevents one from keeping it up. That's all that can be said about land.

JACK: I have a country house with some land, of course, attached to it, about fifteen hundred acres, I believe; but I don't depend on that for my real income. In fact, as far as I can make out, the poachers are the only people who make anything out of it.

LADY BRACKNELL: A country house! How many bedrooms? Well, that point can be cleared up afterwards. You have a town house, I hope? A girl with a simple, unspoiled nature, like Gwendolen, could hardly be expected to reside in the country.

JACK: Well, I own a house in Belgrave Square, but it is let by the year to Lady Bloxham. Of course, I can get it back whenever I like, at six months' notice.

LADY BRACKNELL: Lady Bloxham? I don't know her.

JACK: Oh, she goes about very little. She is a lady considerably advanced in years.

▷ **1** *reproachful:* expressing annoyance or criticism **12** *eligible* ['elɪdʒəbl]: suitable for marriage due to wealth or family background **15** *affectionate* [ə'fekʃənət]: loving **19** *idle* ['aɪdl]: lazy **27** *tamper with sth.:* interfere with sth. **28** *bloom* (n): flower **29** *radically unsound:* without a serious basis, not well-thought out **32** *Grosvenor Square* ['greʊvnə]: upper-class area of London **38** *what between …:* what with … **39–40** *duties exacted after death:* Erbschaftsteuer **44** *acre* ['eɪkə]: ca. 405 m^2 of land **45** *poacher:* person who illegally hunts animals **51** *Belgrave Square:* upper-class area of London

Lady Bracknell: Ah, nowadays that is no guarantee of respectability of character. What number in Belgrave Square?

Jack: 149.

Lady Bracknell: [*Shaking her head.*] The unfashionable side. I thought there was something. However, that could easily be altered.

Jack: Do you mean the fashion, or the side?

Lady Bracknell: [*Sternly.*] Both, if necessary, I presume. What are your politics?

Jack: Well, I am afraid I really have none. I am a Liberal Unionist.

Lady Bracknell: Oh, they count as Tories. They dine with us. Or come in the evening, at any rate. Now to minor matters. Are your parents living?

Jack: I have lost both my parents.

Lady Bracknell: To lose one parent, Mr Worthing, may be regarded as a misfortune; to lose both looks like carelessness. Who was your father? He was evidently a man of some wealth. Was he born in what the Radical papers call the purple of commerce, or did he rise from the ranks of the aristocracy?

Jack: I am afraid I really don't know. The fact is, Lady Bracknell, I said I had lost my parents. It would be nearer the truth to say that my parents seem to have lost me ... I don't actually know who I am by birth. I was ... well, I was found.

Lady Bracknell: Found!

Jack: The late Mr Thomas Cardew, an old gentleman of a very charitable and kindly disposition, found me, and gave me the name of Worthing, because he happened to have a first-class ticket for Worthing in his pocket at the time. Worthing is a place in Sussex. It is a seaside resort.

Lady Bracknell: Where did the charitable gentleman who had a first-class ticket for this seaside resort find you?

JACK: [*Gravely.*] In a hand-bag.

LADY BRACKNELL: A hand-bag?

JACK: [*Very seriously.*] Yes, Lady Bracknell. I was in a hand-bag – a somewhat large, black leather hand-bag, with handles to it – an ordinary hand-bag in fact.

LADY BRACKNELL: In what locality did this Mr James, or Thomas, Cardew come across this ordinary hand-bag?

JACK: In the cloak-room at Victoria Station. It was given to him in mistake for his own.

LADY BRACKNELL: The cloak-room at Victoria Station?

JACK: Yes. The Brighton line.

LADY BRACKNELL: The line is immaterial. Mr Worthing, I confess I feel somewhat bewildered by what you have just told me. To be born, or at any rate bred, in a hand-bag, whether it had handles or not, seems to me to display a contempt for the ordinary decencies of family life that reminds one of the worst excesses of the French Revolution. And I presume you know what that unfortunate movement led to? As for the particular locality in which the hand-bag was found, a cloak-room at a railway station might serve to conceal a social indiscretion – has probably, indeed, been used for that purpose before now – but it could hardly be regarded as an assured basis for a recognised position in good society.

JACK: May I ask you then what you would advise me to do? I need hardly say I would do anything in the world to ensure Gwendolen's happiness.

▷ **10** *Liberal Unionist:* member of the Liberal Party who left the party when the Liberals supported Irish Home Rule; the Liberal Unionists later joined the Conservative Party **11** *Tory:* member of the Conservative Party **18** *purple of commerce:* very wealthy merchant class **25** *late:* (here) no longer alive **26** *kindly disposition:* gentle and generous character **39** *cloak-room:* left-luggage office **42** *line:* (Eisenbahn)strecke **43** *immaterial:* irrelevant **46** *display a contempt for sth.:* show no respect for sth. • *the decencies* ['di:sensiz]: standards of behaviour in society that people think acceptable

Lady Bracknell: I would strongly advise you, Mr Worthing, to try and acquire some relations as soon as possible, and to make a definite effort to produce at any rate one parent, of either sex, before the season is quite over.

Jack: Well, I don't see how I could possibly manage to do that. I can produce the hand-bag at any moment. It is in my dressing-room at home. I really think that should satisfy you, Lady Bracknell.

Lady Bracknell: Me, sir! What has it to do with me? You can hardly imagine that I and Lord Bracknell would dream of allowing our only daughter – a girl brought up with the utmost care – to marry into a cloak-room, and form an alliance with a parcel? Good morning, Mr Worthing!

[Lady Bracknell *sweeps out in majestic indignation.*]

Jack: Good morning! [Algernon, *from the other room, strikes up the Wedding March.* Jack *looks perfectly furious, and goes to the door.*] For goodness' sake don't play that ghastly tune, Algy! How idiotic you are!

[*The music stops and* Algernon *enters cheerily.*]

Algernon: Didn't it go off all right, old boy? You don't mean to say Gwendolen refused you? I know it is a way she has. She is always refusing people. I think it is most ill-natured of her.

Jack: Oh, Gwendolen is as right as a trivet. As far as she is concerned, we are engaged. Her mother is perfectly unbearable. Never met such a Gorgon ... I don't really know what a Gorgon is like, but I am quite sure that Lady Bracknell is one. In any case, she is a monster, without being a myth, which is rather unfair ... I beg your pardon, Algy, I suppose I shouldn't talk about your own aunt in that way before you.

Algernon: My dear boy, I love hearing my relations abused. It is the only thing that makes me put up with them at all. Relations are simply a tedious pack of people, who haven't got the remotest knowledge of how to live, nor the smallest instinct about when to die.

JACK: Oh, that is nonsense!

ALGERNON: It isn't!

JACK: Well, I won't argue about the matter. You always want to argue about things.

ALGERNON: That is exactly what things were originally made for.

JACK: Upon my word, if I thought that, I'd shoot myself ... [*A pause.*] You don't think there is any chance of Gwendolen becoming like her mother in about a hundred and fifty years, do you, Algy?

ALGERNON: All women become like their mothers. That is their tragedy. No man does. That's his.

JACK: Is that clever?

ALGERNON: It is perfectly phrased! and quite as true as any observation in civilized life should be.

JACK: I am sick to death of cleverness. Everybody is clever nowadays. You can't go anywhere without meeting clever people. The thing has become an absolute public nuisance. I wish to goodness we had a few fools left.

ALGERNON: We have.

JACK: I should extremely like to meet them. What do they talk about?

ALGERNON: The fools? Oh! about the clever people, of course.

JACK: What fools!

ALGERNON: By the way, did you tell Gwendolen the truth about your being Ernest in town, and Jack in the country?

▷ **3** *of either sex:* either male or female **13** *sweep out:* leave the room in a quick and exaggerated manner • *in majestic indignation:* showing serious and complete offense **14** *strike sth. up:* (here) play sth. on the piano **15** *the Wedding March:* tune by Felix Mendelssohn (1809–1847) traditionally played at weddings **16** *ghastly* ['gɑːstli]: dreadful **18** *cheerily:* happily **22** *as right as a trivet:* absolutely fine **24** *Gorgon:* mythological monster, with snakes for hair, that turned people into stone **30** *put up with sb./sth.:* tolerate sb./sth. **31–32** *remotest knowledge:* slightest idea **49** *public nuisance:* person who annoys many people

Jack: [*In a very patronizing manner.*] My dear fellow, the truth isn't quite the sort of thing one tells to a nice sweet refined girl. What extraordinary ideas you have about the way to behave to a woman!

Algernon: The only way to behave to a woman is to make love to her, if she is pretty, and to someone else if she is plain.

Jack: Oh, that is nonsense.

Algernon: What about your brother? What about the profligate Ernest?

Jack: Oh, before the end of the week I shall have got rid of him. I'll say he died in Paris of apoplexy. Lots of people die of apoplexy, quite suddenly, don't they?

Algernon: Yes, but it's hereditary, my dear fellow. It's a sort of thing that runs in families. You had much better say a severe chill.

Jack: You are sure a severe chill isn't hereditary, or anything of that kind?

Algernon: Of course it isn't!

Jack: Very well, then. My poor brother Ernest is carried off suddenly, in Paris, by a severe chill. That gets rid of him.

Algernon: But I thought you said that … Miss Cardew was a little too much interested in your poor brother Ernest? Won't she feel his loss a good deal?

Jack: Oh, that is all right. Cecily is not a silly romantic girl, I am glad to say. She has got a capital appetite, goes long walks, and pays no attention at all to her lessons.

Algernon: I would rather like to see Cecily.

Jack: I will take very good care you never do. She is excessively pretty, and she is only just eighteen.

Algernon: Have you told Gwendolen yet that you have an excessively pretty ward who is only just eighteen?

JACK: Oh! one doesn't blurt these things out to people. Cecily and Gwendolen are perfectly certain to be extremely great friends. I'll bet you anything you like that half an hour after they have met, they will be calling each other sister.

ALGERNON: Women only do that when they have called each other a lot of other things first. Now, my dear boy, if we want to get a good table at Willis's, we really must go and dress. Do you know it is nearly seven?

JACK: [*Irritably.*] Oh! It always is nearly seven.

ALGERNON: Well, I'm hungry.

JACK: I never knew you when you weren't ...

ALGERNON: What shall we do after dinner? Go to a theatre?

JACK: Oh no! I loathe listening.

ALGERNON: Well, let us go to the Club?

JACK: Oh, no! I hate talking.

ALGERNON: Well, we might trot round to the Empire at ten?

JACK: Oh, no! I can't bear looking at things. It is so silly.

ALGERNON: Well, what shall we do?

JACK: Nothing!

ALGERNON: It is awfully hard work doing nothing. However, I don't mind hard work where there is no definite object of any kind.

[*Enter* LANE.]

LANE: Miss Fairfax.

▷ **1** *patronize sb.:* show that you are superior to or know more than sb. **7** *profligate* ['prɒflɪgət]: extravagant, lacking in morals **10** *apoplexy* ['æpəpleksi]: Schlaganfall **23** *capital* (adj): large, great **29** *ward* (n): Mündel **30** *blurt sth. out:* say sth. indiscreet without meaning to **36** dress (v): (here) put on an evening suit **38** *irritably:* in an annoyed or angry manner **42** *loathe sth.* [ləʊð]: hate sth. **45** *the Empire:* a London theatre which offered light entertainment

[*Enter* GWENDOLEN. LANE *goes out.*]

ALGERNON: Gwendolen, upon my word!

GWENDOLEN: Algy, kindly turn your back. I have something very particular to say to Mr Worthing.

ALGERNON: Really, Gwendolen, I don't think I can allow this at all.

GWENDOLEN: Algy, you always adopt a strictly immoral attitude towards life. You are not quite old enough to do that. [ALGERNON *retires to the fireplace.*]

JACK: My own darling!

GWENDOLEN: Ernest, we may never be married. From the expression on mamma's face I fear we never shall. Few parents nowadays pay any regard to what their children say to them. The old-fashioned respect for the young is fast dying out. Whatever influence I ever had over mamma, I lost at the age of three. But although she may prevent us from becoming man and wife, and I may marry someone else, and marry often, nothing that she can possibly do can alter my eternal devotion to you.

JACK: Dear Gwendolen!

GWENDOLEN: The story of your romantic origin, as related to me by mamma, with unpleasing comments, has naturally stirred the deeper fibres of my nature. Your Christian name has an irresistible fascination. The simplicity of your character makes you exquisitely incomprehensible to me. Your town address at the Albany I have. What is your address in the country?

JACK: The Manor House, Woolton, Hertfordshire.

[ALGERNON, *who has been carefully listening, smiles to himself, and writes the address on his shirt-cuff. Then picks up the Railway Guide.*]

GWENDOLEN: There is a good postal service, I suppose? It may be necessary to do something desperate. That of course will require serious consideration. I will communicate with you daily.

JACK: My own one!

GWENDOLEN: How long do you remain in town?

JACK: Till Monday.

GWENDOLEN: Good! Algy, you may turn round now.

ALGERNON: Thanks, I've turned round already.

GWENDOLEN: You may also ring the bell.

[ALGERNON *rings bell.*]

JACK: You will let me see you to your carriage, my own darling?

GWENDOLEN: Certainly.

[*Enter* LANE.]

JACK: I will see Miss Fairfax out.

LANE: Yes, sir.

[JACK *and* GWENDOLEN *go off.* LANE *presents several letters on a salver to* ALGERNON. *It is to be surmised that they are bills, as* ALGERNON, *after looking at the envelopes, tears them up.]*

ALGERNON: A glass of sherry, Lane.

LANE: Yes, sir.

ALGERNON: Tomorrow, Lane, I'm going Bunburying.

LANE: Yes, sir.

ALGERNON: I shall probably not be back till Monday. You can put up my dress clothes, my smoking jacket, and all the Bunbury suits . . .

▷ **17** *eternal:* everlasting • *devotion*: love, affection and loyalty **21** *deeper fibres:* (here) innermost parts **22–23** *exquisite:* delightful, wonderful **23** *incomprehensible:* that cannot be understood **25** *Hertfordshire* ['hɑːtfədʃə]: county (= Grafschaft) north of London **27** *shirt-cuff:* Manschette **27–28** *the Railway Guide:* book containing the railway timetable **45** *surmise sth.:* assume sth. **51** *put sth. up* (old use): prepare sth. **52** *dress clothes:* smart clothes for formal occasions • *smoking jacket:* Hausjacke

LANE: Yes, sir. [*Handing sherry.*]

ALGERNON: I hope tomorrow will be a fine day, Lane.

LANE: It never is, sir.

ALGERNON: Lane, you're a perfect pessimist.

LANE: I do my best to give satisfaction, sir.

[*Enter* JACK. LANE *goes off.*]

JACK: There's a sensible, intellectual girl! the only girl I ever cared for in my life. [ALGERNON *is laughing immoderately.*] What on earth are you so amused at?

ALGERNON: Oh, I'm a little anxious about poor Bunbury, that is all.

JACK: If you don't take care, your friend Bunbury will get you into a serious scrape some day.

ALGERNON: I love scrapes. They are the only things that are never serious.

JACK: Oh, that's nonsense, Algy. You never talk anything but nonsense.

ALGERNON: Nobody ever does.

[JACK *looks indignantly at him, and leaves the room.* ALGERNON *lights a cigarette, reads his shirt-cuff, and smiles.*]

ACT DROP

SECOND ACT

Scene: Garden at the Manor House. A flight of grey stone steps leads up to the house. The garden, an old-fashioned one, full of roses. Time of year, July. Basket chairs, and a table covered with books, are set under a large yew-tree.
MISS PRISM *discovered seated at the table.* CECILY *is at the back watering flowers.*

MISS PRISM: [*Calling.*] Cecily, Cecily! Surely such a utilitarian occupation as the watering of flowers is rather Moulton's duty than yours? Especially at a moment when intellectual pleasures await you. Your German grammar is on the table. Pray open it at page fifteen. We will repeat yesterday's lesson.

CECILY: [*Coming over very slowly.*] But I don't like German. It isn't at all a becoming language. I know perfectly well that I look quite plain after my German lesson.

MISS PRISM: Child, you know how anxious your guardian is that you should improve yourself in every way. He laid particular stress on your German, as he was leaving for town yesterday. Indeed, he always lays stress on your German when he is leaving for town.

CECILY: Dear Uncle Jack is so very serious! Sometimes he is so serious that I think he cannot be quite well.

MISS PRISM: [*Drawing herself up.*] Your guardian enjoys the best of health, and his gravity of demeanour is especially to be commended in one so comparatively young as he is. I know no one who has a higher sense of duty and responsibility.

▷ **8** *immoderately:* in an exaggerated manner **18** *indignant:* angry **20** *act drop:* the curtain closes **27** *utilitarian* [juˌtɪlɪ'teəriən]: practical **28** *Moulton:* a gardener (who does not appear on stage) **33** *becoming* (adj): making sb. feel attractive **34** *plain:* ordinary **35** *be anxious that …:* (here) want very much … **42** *gravity of demeanour* [dɪ'mi:nə]: serious way of behaving or looking **43** *commend sth.:* (here) admire sth.

Cecily: I suppose that is why he often looks a little bored when we three are together.

Miss Prism: Cecily! I am surprised at you. Mr Worthing has many troubles in his life. Idle merriment and triviality would be out of place in his conversation. You must remember his constant anxiety about that unfortunate young man his brother.

Cecily: I wish Uncle Jack would allow that unfortunate young man, his brother, to come down here sometimes. We might have a good influence over him, Miss Prism. I am sure you certainly would. You know German, and geology, and things of that kind influence a man very much. [Cecily *begins to write in her diary.*]

Miss Prism: [*Shaking her head.*] I do not think that even I could produce any effect on a character that according to his own brother's admission is irretrievably weak and vacillating. Indeed I am not sure that I would desire to reclaim him. I am not in favour of this modern mania for turning bad people into good people at a moment's notice. As a man sows so let him reap. You must put away your diary, Cecily. I really don't see why you should keep a diary at all.

Cecily: I keep a diary in order to enter the wonderful secrets of my life. If I didn't write them down, I should probably forget all about them.

Miss Prism: Memory, my dear Cecily, is the diary that we all carry about with us.

Cecily: Yes, but it usually chronicles the things that have never happened, and couldn't possibly have happened. I believe that Memory is responsible for nearly all the three-volume novels that Mudie sends us.

Miss Prism: Do not speak slightingly of the three-volume novel, Cecily. I wrote one myself in earlier days.

Cecily: Did you really, Miss Prism? How wonderfully clever you are! I hope it did not end happily? I don't like novels that end happily. They depress me so much.

MISS PRISM: The good ended happily, and the bad unhappily. That is what Fiction means.

CECILY: I suppose so. But it seems very unfair. And was your novel ever published?

MISS PRISM: Alas! no. The manuscript unfortunately was abandoned. [CECILY *starts.*] I use the word in the sense of lost or mislaid. To your work, child, these speculations are profitless.

CECILY: [*Smiling.*] But I see dear Dr Chasuble coming up through the garden.

MISS PRISM: [*Rising and advancing.*] Dr Chasuble! This is indeed a pleasure.

[*Enter* CANON CHASUBLE.]

CHASUBLE: And how are we this morning? Miss Prism, you are, I trust, well?

CECILY: Miss Prism has just been complaining of a slight headache. I think it would do her so much good to have a short stroll with you in the Park, Dr Chasuble.

MISS PRISM: Cecily, I have not mentioned anything about a headache.

CECILY: No, dear Miss Prism, I know that, but I felt instinctively that you had a headache. Indeed I was thinking about that, and not about my German lesson, when the Rector came in.

CHASUBLE: I hope, Cecily, you are not inattentive.

▷ **4** *idle merriment:* (here) worthless entertainment **14** *admission:* statement in which a person accepts that sth. (usu. bad) is true • *irretrievable* [ˌɪrɪ'triːvəbl]: unwiederbringlich • *vacillating:* (here) unable to decide what to do **15** *reclaim sb.:* (here) help sb. become a good person **16** *mania for sth.:* strong wish for sth. / to do sth. **16–17** *at a moment's notice:* in a very short time **17** *sow sth.:* etwas säen • *reap sth.:* etwas ernten **25** *chronicle sth.* ['krɒnɪkl]: (here) record sth. **28** *Mudie:* a mobile library service which offered many 'conservative' novels in the 1890s **29** *speak slightingly of sb./sth.:* talk about sb./sth. in a negative way **38** *abandon sth.:* stop writing sth.; leave sth. somewhere **40** *be profitless:* have no use **49** *stroll* (n): peaceful walk **54** *rector:* (in the Church of England) clergyman in charge of a parish

CECILY: Oh, I am afraid I am.

CHASUBLE: That is strange. Were I fortunate enough to be Miss Prism's pupil, I would hang upon her lips. [MISS PRISM *glares.*] I spoke metaphorically. – My metaphor was drawn from bees. Ahem! Mr Worthing, I suppose, has not returned from town yet?

MISS PRISM: We do not expect him till Monday afternoon.

CHASUBLE: Ah yes, he usually likes to spend his Sunday in London. He is not one of those whose sole aim is enjoyment, as, by all accounts, that unfortunate young man his brother seems to be. But I must not disturb Egeria and her pupil any longer.

MISS PRISM: Egeria? My name is Laetitia, Doctor.

CHASUBLE: [*Bowing.*] A classical allusion merely, drawn from the Pagan authors. I shall see you both no doubt at Evensong?

MISS PRISM: I think, dear Doctor, I will have a stroll with you. I find I have a headache after all, and a walk might do it good.

CHASUBLE: With pleasure, Miss Prism, with pleasure. We might go as far as the schools and back.

MISS PRISM: That would be delightful. Cecily, you will read your Political Economy in my absence. The chapter on the Fall of the Rupee you may omit. It is somewhat too sensational. Even these metallic problems have their melodramatic side.

[*Goes down the garden with* Dr CHASUBLE.]

CECILY: [*Picks up books and throws them back on table.*] Horrid Political Economy! Horrid Geography! Horrid, horrid German!

[*Enter* MERRIMAN *with a card on a salver.*]

MERRIMAN: Mr Ernest Worthing has just driven over from the station. He has brought his luggage with him.

CECILY: [*Takes the card and reads it.*] 'Mr Ernest Worthing, B. 4, The Albany, W.' Uncle Jack's brother! Did you tell him Mr Worthing was in town?

MERRIMAN: Yes, Miss. He seemed very much disappointed. I mentioned that you and Miss Prism were in the garden. He said he was anxious to speak to you privately for a moment.

CECILY: Ask Mr Ernest Worthing to come here. I suppose you had better talk to the housekeeper about a room for him.

MERRIMAN: Yes, Miss.

[MERRIMAN *goes off.*]

CECILY: I have never met any really wicked person before. I feel rather frightened. I am so afraid he will look just like every one else.

[*Enter* ALGERNON, *very gay and debonair.*]

He does!

ALGERNON: [*Raising his hat.*] You are my little cousin Cecily, I'm sure.

CECILY: You are under some strange mistake. I am not little. In fact, I believe I am more than usually tall for my age. [ALGERNON *is rather taken aback.*] But I am your cousin Cecily. You, I see from your card, are Uncle Jack's brother, my cousin Ernest, my wicked cousin Ernest.

ALGERNON: Oh! I am not really wicked at all, cousin Cecily. You mustn't think that I am wicked.

CECILY: If you are not, then you have certainly been deceiving us all in a very inexcusable manner. I hope you have not been leading a double life, pretending to be wicked and being really good all the time. That would be hypocrisy.

▷ **3** *glare* (v): look or stare in an angry way **8** *sole:* only **10** *Egeria* [ɪˈdʒɪəriə]: (in Roman mythology) a nymph who was advisor to a king before becoming his lover **11** *Laetitia* [lɪˈtɪʃə] (Latin) happiness **13** *pagan* [ˈpeɪgn]: (here) Greek and Roman • *Evensong* [ˈiːvənsɒŋ]: (in der anglikanischen Kirche) Abendandacht **19** *Fall:* Absturz **20** *rupee:* Indian currency **40** *gay:* happy, joyful • *debonair* [ˌdebəˈneə]: fashionable, refined and confident **45–46** *rather taken aback*: slightly surprised

ALGERNON: [*Looks at her in amazement.*] Oh! Of course I have been rather reckless.

CECILY: I am glad to hear it.

ALGERNON: In fact, now you mention the subject, I have been very bad in my own small way.

CECILY: I don't think you should be so proud of that, though I am sure it must have been very pleasant.

ALGERNON: It is much pleasanter being here with you.

CECILY: I can't understand how you are here at all. Uncle Jack won't be back till Monday afternoon.

ALGERNON: That is a great disappointment. I am obliged to go up by the first train on Monday morning. I have a business appointment that I am anxious ... to miss!

CECILY: Couldn't you miss it anywhere but in London?

ALGERNON: No: the appointment is in London.

CECILY: Well, I know, of course, how important it is not to keep a business engagement, if one wants to retain any sense of the beauty of life, but still I think you had better wait till Uncle Jack arrives. I know he wants to speak to you about your emigrating.

ALGERNON: About my what?

CECILY: Your emigrating. He has gone up to buy your outfit.

ALGERNON: I certainly wouldn't let Jack buy my outfit. He has no taste in neckties at all.

CECILY: I don't think you will require neckties. Uncle Jack is sending you to Australia.

ALGERNON: Australia! I'd sooner die.

CECILY: Well, he said at dinner on Wednesday night, that you would have to choose between this world, the next world, and Australia.

ALGERNON: Oh, well! The accounts I have received of Australia and the next world are not particularly encouraging. This world is good enough for me, cousin Cecily.

CECILY: Yes, but are you good enough for it?

ALGERNON: I'm afraid I'm not that. That is why I want you to reform me. You might make that your mission, if you don't mind, cousin Cecily.

CECILY: I'm afraid I've no time, this afternoon.

ALGERNON: Well, would you mind my reforming myself this afternoon?

CECILY: It is rather Quixotic of you. But I think you should try.

ALGERNON: I will. I feel better already.

CECILY: You are looking a little worse.

ALGERNON: That is because I am hungry.

CECILY: How thoughtless of me. I should have remembered that when one is going to lead an entirely new life, one requires regular and wholesome meals. Won't you come in?

ALGERNON: Thank you. Might I have a buttonhole first? I never have any appetite unless I have a buttonhole first.

CECILY: A Maréchal Niel? [*Picks up scissors.*]

ALGERNON: No, I'd sooner have a pink rose.

CECILY: Why? [*Cuts a flower.*]

ALGERNON: Because you are like a pink rose, Cousin Cecily.

▷ **2** *reckless:* careless, irresponsible **13** *be anxious to miss sth.:* want to avoid sth. very much **14** *anywhere but in London:* anderswo als in London **22** *outfit:* (here) clothes (for travelling) **34** *mission:* (here) Lebensaufgabe **39** *Quixotic* [kwɪk'sɒtɪk]: idealistic in a way that is too unrealistic **47** *buttonhole:* (here) flower worn in a buttonhole **48** *Maréchal Niel* [ˌmɑːrəʃæl 'njəl]: a yellow rose

CECILY: I don't think it can be right for you to talk to me like that. Miss Prism never says such things to me.

ALGERNON: Then Miss Prism is a short-sighted old lady. [CECILY *puts the rose in his buttonhole.*] You are the prettiest girl I ever saw.

CECILY: Miss Prism says that all good looks are a snare.

ALGERNON: They are a snare that every sensible man would like to be caught in.

CECILY: Oh! I don't think I would care to catch a sensible man. I shouldn't know what to talk to him about.

[*They pass into the house.* MISS PRISM *and* DR CHASUBLE *return.*]

MISS PRISM: You are too much alone, dear Dr Chasuble. You should get married. A misanthrope I can understand – a womanthrope, never!

CHASUBLE: [*With a scholar's shudder.*] Believe me, I do not deserve so neologistic a phrase. The precept as well as the practice of the Primitive Church was distinctly against matrimony.

MISS PRISM: [*Sententiously.*] That is obviously the reason why the Primitive Church has not lasted up to the present day. And you do not seem to realize, dear Doctor, that by persistently remaining single, a man converts himself into a permanent public temptation. Men should be more careful; this very celibacy leads weaker vessels astray.

CHASUBLE: But is a man not equally attractive when married?

MISS PRISM: No married man is ever attractive except to his wife.

CHASUBLE: And often, I've been told, not even to her.

MISS PRISM: That depends on the intellectual sympathies of the woman. Maturity can always be depended on. Ripeness can be trusted. Young women are green. [DR CHASUBLE *starts.*] I spoke horticulturally. My metaphor was drawn from fruits. But where is Cecily?

Chasuble: Perhaps she followed us to the schools.

[*Enter* Jack *slowly from the back of the garden. He is dressed in the deepest mourning, with crape hatband and black gloves.*]

Miss Prism: Mr Worthing!

Chasuble: Mr Worthing?

Miss Prism: This is indeed a surprise. We did not look for you till Monday afternoon.

Jack: [*Shakes* Miss Prism*'s hand in a tragic manner.*] I have returned sooner than I expected. Dr Chasuble, I hope you are well?

Chasuble: Dear Mr Worthing, I trust this garb of woe does not betoken some terrible calamity?

Jack: My brother.

Miss Prism: More shameful debts and extravagance?

Chasuble: Still leading his life of pleasure?

Jack: [*Shaking his head.*] Dead!

Chasuble: Your brother Ernest dead?

Jack: Quite dead.

Miss Prism: What a lesson for him! I trust he will profit by it.

▷ **5** *snare* (n): trap **6** *sensible:* intelligent, reasonable **12** *misanthrope* ['mɪsənθrəʊp]: person who hates other people • *womanthrope:* (word created by Miss Prism) person who hates women **14** *a scholar's shudder:* der Schauder eines Gelehrten **15** *neologistic* [nɪˌəlɒ'dʒɪstɪk]: (of a word) newly created • *precept* ['pri:sept]: rule, law **15–16** *the Primitive Church:* the early church (i.e. in the first centuries AD) **16** *matrimony:* marriage **21** *celibacy:* Ehelosigkeit, Zölibat **21–22** *lead sb. astray:* teach sb. bad ways or habits **21–22** *weaker vessel:* (esp. in Christianity) woman **26** *sympathies:* (here) interests **29** *horticulturally:* (here) in terms of garden plants **33** *crape hatband* [kreɪp]: Trauerflor am Hut **36** *look for sb.:* (here) expect sb. **41** *garb of woe* [wəʊ]: (here) black clothes worn to mark sb.'s death **42** *betoken sth.* (fml): mean sth., indicate sth. • *calamity:* catastrophe, terrible event

Chasuble: Mr Worthing, I offer you my sincere condolence. You have at least the consolation of knowing that you were always the most generous and forgiving of brothers.

Jack: Poor Ernest! He had many faults, but it is a sad, sad blow.

Chasuble: Very sad indeed. Were you with him at the end?

Jack: No. He died abroad; in Paris, in fact. I had a telegram last night from the manager of the Grand Hotel.

Chasuble: Was the cause of death mentioned?

Jack: A severe chill, it seems.

Miss Prism: As a man sows, so shall he reap.

Chasuble: [*Raising his hand.*] Charity, dear Miss Prism, charity! None of us are perfect. I myself am peculiarly susceptible to draughts. Will the interment take place here?

Jack: No. He seems to have expressed a desire to be buried in Paris.

Chasuble: In Paris! [*Shakes his head.*] I fear that hardly points to any very serious state of mind at the last. You would no doubt wish me to make some slight allusion to this tragic domestic affliction next Sunday. [Jack *presses his hand convulsively.*] My sermon on the meaning of the manna in the wilderness can be adapted to almost any occasion, joyful, or, as in the present case, distressing. [*All sigh.*] I have preached it at harvest celebrations, christenings, confirmations, on days of humiliation and festal days. The last time I delivered it was in the Cathedral, as a charity sermon on behalf of the Society for the Prevention of Discontent among the Upper Orders. The Bishop, who was present, was much struck by some of the analogies I drew.

Jack: Ah! that reminds me, you mentioned christenings I think, Dr. Chasuble? I suppose you know how to christen all right? [Dr Chasuble *looks astounded.*] I mean, of course, you are continually christening, aren't you?

MISS PRISM: It is, I regret to say, one of the Rector's most constant duties in this parish. I have often spoken to the poorer classes on the subject. But they don't seem to know what thrift is.

CHASUBLE: But is there any particular infant in whom you are interested, Mr Worthing? Your brother was, I believe, unmarried, was he not?

JACK: Oh yes.

MISS PRISM: [*Bitterly.*] People who live entirely for pleasure usually are.

JACK: But it is not for any child, dear Doctor. I am very fond of children. No! the fact is, I would like to be christened myself, this afternoon, if you have nothing better to do.

CHASUBLE: But surely, Mr Worthing, you have been christened already?

JACK: I don't remember anything about it.

CHASUBLE: But have you any grave doubts on the subject?

JACK: I certainly intend to have. Of course I don't know if the thing would bother you in any way, or if you think I am a little too old now.

CHASUBLE: Not at all. The sprinkling, and, indeed, the immersion of adults is a perfectly canonical practice.

JACK: Immersion!

▷ **1** *offer sb. your condolence:* jdm. sein Beileid ausdrücken **12** *susceptible to sth.* [sə'septəbl]: (here) sensitive to sth., easily affected by sth. **13** *draught* [drɑ:ft]: Luftzug • *internment* (fml): burial, funeral **17** *allusion:* mention, reference • *domestic affliction:* family tragedy **18** *convulsively*: (here) in an exaggerated manner **19** *manna in the wilderness:* (in the Bible) food sent from heaven to the Israelites in the desert **22** *humiliation:* Erniedrigung **26** *draw analogies:* make comparisons **33** *thrift* (n): state of being careful with sth. (esp. money; here, sexual pleasure) and not wasting it **48** *bother sb.*: trouble sb., disturb sb. **50** *sprinkling:* baptism by throwing a little water on the head of a person • *immersion:* baptism by putting the whole body under water **51** *canonical practice:* action permitted by the Church

CHASUBLE: You need have no apprehensions. Sprinkling is all that is necessary, or indeed I think advisable. Our weather is so changeable. At what hour would you wish the ceremony performed?

JACK: Oh, I might trot round about five if that would suit you.

CHASUBLE: Perfectly, perfectly! In fact I have two similar ceremonies to perform at that time. A case of twins that occurred recently in one of the outlying cottages on your own estate. Poor Jenkins the carter, a most hard-working man.

JACK: Oh! I don't see much fun in being christened along with other babies. It would be childish. Would half-past five do?

CHASUBLE: Admirably! Admirably! [*Takes out watch.*] And now, dear Mr Worthing, I will not intrude any longer into a house of sorrow. I would merely beg you not to be too much bowed down by grief. What seem to us bitter trials are often blessings in disguise.

MISS PRISM: This seems to me a blessing of an extremely obvious kind.

[*Enter* CECILY *from the house.*]

CECILY: Uncle Jack! Oh, I am pleased to see you back. But what horrid clothes you have got on! Do go and change them.

MISS PRISM: Cecily!

CHASUBLE: My child! my child! [CECILY *goes towards* JACK; *he kisses her brow in a melancholy manner.*]

CECILY: What is the matter, Uncle Jack? Do look happy! You look as if you had toothache, and I have got such a surprise for you. Who do you think is in the dining-room? Your brother!

JACK: Who?

CECILY: Your brother Ernest. He arrived about half an hour ago.

JACK: What nonsense! I haven't got a brother.

CECILY: Oh, don't say that. However badly he may have behaved to you in the past he is still your brother. You couldn't be so heartless as to disown him. I'll tell him to come out. And you will shake hands with him, won't you, Uncle Jack? [*Runs back into the house.*]

CHASUBLE: These are very joyful tidings.

MISS PRISM: After we had all been resigned to his loss, his sudden return seems to me peculiarly distressing.

JACK: My brother is in the dining-room? I don't know what it all means. I think it is perfectly absurd.

[*Enter* ALGERNON *and* CECILY *hand in hand. They come slowly up to* JACK.]

JACK: Good heavens! [*Motions* ALGERNON *away.*]

ALGERNON: Brother John, I have come down from town to tell you that I am very sorry for all the trouble I have given you, and that I intend to lead a better life in the future. [JACK *glares at him and does not take his hand.*]

CECILY: Uncle Jack, you are not going to refuse your own brother's hand?

JACK: Nothing will induce me to take his hand. I think his coming down here disgraceful. He knows perfectly well why.

CECILY: Uncle Jack, do be nice. There is some good in everyone. Ernest has just been telling me about his poor invalid friend Mr Bunbury whom he goes to visit so often. And surely there must be much good in one who is kind to an invalid, and leaves the pleasures of London to sit by a bed of pain.

JACK: Oh! he has been talking about Bunbury, has he?

CECILY: Yes, he has told me all about poor Mr Bunbury, and his terrible state of health.

▷ **1** *apprehensions:* (here) fears **4** *trot round* (infml): (here) go round to visit sb. for a short time **8** *carter:* person who makes carts **12** *intrude into sth.* (fml): (here) disturb sth. **14** *bitter trials* (fml): (here) painful difficulties • *be blessings in disguise:* sich im Nachhinein als gut herausstellen **30** *disown sb.:* reject sb., have nothing to do with sb. **33** *tidings* (pl; fml): news **40** *motion sb. away:* give a sign to sb. to go away

JACK: Bunbury! Well, I won't have him talk to you about Bunbury or about anything else. It is enough to drive one perfectly frantic.

ALGERNON: Of course I admit that the faults were all on my side. But I must say that I think that Brother John's coldness to me is peculiarly painful. I expected a more enthusiastic welcome, especially considering it is the first time I have come here.

CECILY: Uncle Jack, if you don't shake hands with Ernest I will never forgive you.

JACK: Never forgive me?

CECILY: Never, never, never!

JACK: Well, this is the last time I shall ever do it. [*Shakes with* ALGERNON *and glares.*]

CHASUBLE: It's pleasant, is it not, to see so perfect a reconciliation? I think we might leave the two brothers together.

MISS PRISM: Cecily, you will come with us.

CECILY: Certainly, Miss Prism. My little task of reconciliation is over.

CHASUBLE: You have done a beautiful action today, dear child.

MISS PRISM: We must not be premature in our judgments.

CECILY: I feel very happy.

[*They all go off except* JACK *and* ALGERNON.]

JACK: You young scoundrel, Algy, you must get out of this place as soon as possible. I don't allow any Bunburying here.

[*Enter* MERRIMAN.]

MERRIMAN: I have put Mr Ernest's things in the room next to yours, sir. I suppose that is all right?

JACK: What?

MERRIMAN: Mr Ernest's luggage, sir. I have unpacked it and put it in the room next to your own.

JACK: His luggage?

MERRIMAN: Yes, sir. Three portmanteaus, a dressing-case, two hatboxes, and a large luncheon-basket.

ALGERNON: I am afraid I can't stay more than a week this time.

JACK: Merriman, order the dog-cart at once. Mr Ernest has been suddenly called back to town.

MERRIMAN: Yes, sir. [*Goes back into the house.*]

ALGERNON: What a fearful liar you are, Jack. I have not been called back to town at all.

JACK: Yes, you have.

ALGERNON: I haven't heard anyone call me.

JACK: Your duty as a gentleman calls you back.

ALGERNON: My duty as a gentleman has never interfered with my pleasures in the smallest degree.

JACK: I can quite understand that.

ALGERNON: Well, Cecily is a darling.

JACK: You are not to talk of Miss Cardew like that. I don't like it.

ALGERNON: Well, I don't like your clothes. You look perfectly ridiculous in them. Why on earth don't you go up and change? It is perfectly childish to be in deep mourning for a man who is actually staying for a whole week with you in your house as a guest. I call it grotesque.

▷ **18** *premature* ['premətʃə]: happening too quickly or early **21** *scoundrel* ['skaʊdrəl]: Schurke **30** *portmanteau* [pɔːt'mæntəʊ]: Schrankkoffer • *dressing-case:* travelling case for brushes, cologne bottles, soap, etc. **33** *dog-cart:* small, two-wheeled cart pulled by a horse **36** *fearful:* (here) terrible **41** *interfere with sth.:* (here) interrupt sth., spoil sth. **48** *be in mourning* ['mɔːnɪŋ]: wear black clothes when a person has died

JACK: You are certainly not staying with me for a whole week as a guest or anything else. You have got to leave ... by the four-five train.

ALGERNON: I certainly won't leave you so long as you are in mourning. It would be most unfriendly. If I were in mourning you would stay with me, I suppose. I should think it very unkind if you didn't.

JACK: Well, will you go if I change my clothes?

ALGERNON: Yes, if you are not too long. I never saw anybody take so long to dress, and with such little result.

JACK: Well, at any rate, that is better than being always over-dressed as you are.

ALGERNON: If I am occasionally a little over-dressed, I make up for it by being always immensely over-educated.

JACK: Your vanity is ridiculous, your conduct an outrage, and your presence in my garden utterly absurd. However, you have got to catch the four-five, and I hope you will have a pleasant journey back to town. This Bunburying, as you call it, has not been a great success for you.

[*Goes into the house.*]

ALGERNON: I think it has been a great success. I'm in love with Cecily, and that is everything.

[*Enter* CECILY *at the back of the garden. She picks up the can and begins to water the flowers.*]

But I must see her before I go, and make arrangements for another Bunbury. Ah, there she is.

CECILY: Oh, I merely came back to water the roses. I thought you were with Uncle Jack.

ALGERNON: He's gone to order the dog-cart for me.

CECILY: Oh, is he going to take you for a nice drive?

ALGERNON: He's going to send me away.

CECILY: Then have we got to part?

ALGERNON: I am afraid so. It's a very painful parting.

CECILY: It is always painful to part from people whom one has known for a very brief space of time. The absence of old friends one can endure with equanimity. But even a momentary separation from anyone to whom one has just been introduced is almost unbearable.

ALGERNON: Thank you.

[*Enter* MERRIMAN.]

MERRIMAN: The dog-cart is at the door, sir.

[ALGERNON *looks appealingly at* CECILY.]

CECILY: It can wait, Merriman ... for ... five minutes.

MERRIMAN: Yes, Miss. [*Exit* MERRIMAN.]

ALGERNON: I hope, Cecily, I shall not offend you if I state quite frankly and openly that you seem to me to be in every way the visible personification of absolute perfection.

CECILY: I think your frankness does you great credit, Ernest. If you will allow me, I will copy your remarks into my diary. [*Goes over to table and begins writing in diary.*]

ALGERNON: Do you really keep a diary? I'd give anything to look at it. May I?

CECILY: Oh no. [*Puts her hand over it.*] You see, it is simply a very young girl's record of her own thoughts and impressions, and consequently meant for publication. When it appears in volume

▷ **13** *make up for sth.:* etwas wieder gutmachen **15** *outrage* (n): action that shocks people **16** *utterly:* completely **17** *four-five:* (here) train that departs at five minutes past four **36** *endure sth. with equanimity:* tolerate sth. calmly **42** *look appealingly at sb.:* ask sb. for sth. (e.g. help, sympathy) by looking at them **48** *do sb. great credit:* show that sb. has good qualities

form I hope you will order a copy. But pray, Ernest, don't stop. I delight in taking down from dictation. I have reached 'absolute perfection'. You can go on. I am quite ready for more.

ALGERNON: [*Somewhat taken aback.*] Ahem! Ahem!

CECILY: Oh, don't cough, Ernest. When one is dictating one should speak fluently and not cough. Besides, I don't know how to spell a cough. [*Writes as* ALGERNON *speaks.*]

ALGERNON: [*Speaking very rapidly.*] Cecily, ever since I first looked upon your wonderful and incomparable beauty, I have dared to love you wildly, passionately, devotedly, hopelessly.

CECILY: I don't think that you should tell me that you love me wildly, passionately, devotedly, hopelessly. Hopelessly doesn't seem to make much sense, does it?

ALGERNON: Cecily!

[*Enter* MERRIMAN.]

MERRIMAN: The dog-cart is waiting, sir.

ALGERNON: Tell it to come round next week, at the same hour.

MERRIMAN: [*Looks at* CECILY, *who makes no sign.*] Yes, sir.

[MERRIMAN *retires.*]

CECILY: Uncle Jack would be very much annoyed if he knew you were staying on till next week, at the same hour.

ALGERNON: Oh, I don't care about Jack. I don't care for anybody in the whole world but you. I love you, Cecily. You will marry me, won't you?

CECILY: You silly boy! Of course. Why, we have been engaged for the last three months.

ALGERNON: For the last three months?

CECILY: Yes, it will be exactly three months on Thursday.

ALGERNON: But how did we become engaged?

CECILY: Well, ever since dear Uncle Jack first confessed to us that he had a younger brother who was very wicked and bad, you of course have formed the chief topic of conversation between myself and Miss Prism. And of course a man who is much talked about is always very attractive. One feels there must be something in him, after all. I daresay it was foolish of me, but I fell in love with you, Ernest.

ALGERNON: Darling! And when was the engagement actually settled?

CECILY: On the 14th of February last. Worn out by your entire ignorance of my existence, I determined to end the matter one way or the other, and after a long struggle with myself I accepted you under this dear old tree here. The next day I bought this little ring in your name, and this is the little bangle with the true lover's knot I promised you always to wear.

ALGERNON: Did I give you this? It's very pretty, isn't it?

CECILY: Yes, you've wonderfully good taste, Ernest. It's the excuse I've always given for your leading such a bad life. And this is the box in which I keep all your dear letters. [*Kneels at table, opens box, and produces letters tied up with blue ribbon.*]

ALGERNON: My letters! But, my own sweet Cecily, I have never written you any letters.

CECILY: You need hardly remind me of that, Ernest. I remember only too well that I was forced to write your letters for you. I wrote always three times a week, and sometimes oftener.

ALGERNON: Oh, do let me read them, Cecily?

CECILY: Oh, I couldn't possibly. They would make you far too conceited. [*Replaces box.*] The three you wrote me after I had broken off the engagement are so beautiful, and so badly spelled, that even now I can hardly read them without crying a little.

▷ **9** *incomparable:* perfect; that is like no other **35** *I daresay:* (here) perhaps **38** *worn out:* exhausted **42** *bangle* ['bæŋgl]: bracelet **55–56** *conceited* [kən'siːtɪd]: too proud of yourself; arrogant

Algernon: But was our engagement ever broken off?

Cecily: Of course it was. On the 22nd of last March. You can see the entry if you like. [*Shows diary.*] 'Today I broke off my engagement with Ernest. I feel it is better to do so. The weather still continues charming.'

Algernon: But why on earth did you break it off? What had I done? I had done nothing at all. Cecily, I am very much hurt indeed to hear you broke it off. Particularly when the weather was so charming.

Cecily: It would hardly have been a really serious engagement if it hadn't been broken off at least once. But I forgave you before the week was out.

Algernon: [*Crossing to her, and kneeling.*] What a perfect angel you are, Cecily.

Cecily: You dear romantic boy. [*He kisses her, she puts her fingers through his hair.*] I hope your hair curls naturally, does it?

Algernon: Yes, darling, with a little help from others.

Cecily: I am so glad.

Algernon: You'll never break off our engagement again, Cecily?

Cecily: I don't think I could break it off now that I have actually met you. Besides, of course, there is the question of your name.

Algernon: [*Nervously.*] – Yes, of course.

Cecily: You must not laugh at me, darling, but it had always been a girlish dream of mine to love someone whose name was Ernest. [Algernon *rises,* Cecily *also.*] There is something in that name that seems to inspire absolute confidence. I pity any poor married woman whose husband is not called Ernest.

Algernon: But, my dear child, do you mean to say you could not love me if I had some other name?

Cecily: But what name?

Algernon: Oh, any name you like – Algernon – for instance …

Cecily: But I don't like the name of Algernon.

Algernon: Well, my own dear, sweet, loving little darling, I really can't see why you should object to the name of Algernon. It is not at all a bad name. In fact, it is rather an aristocratic name. Half of the chaps who get into the Bankruptcy Court are called Algernon: But seriously, Cecily … [*Moving to her.*] … if my name was Algy, couldn't you love me?

Cecily: [*Rising.*] I might respect you, Ernest, I might admire your character, but I fear that I should not be able to give you my undivided attention.

Algernon: Ahem! Cecily! [*Picking up hat.*] Your Rector here is, I suppose, thoroughly experienced in the practice of all the rites and ceremonials of the Church?

Cecily: Oh, yes. Dr Chasuble is a most learned man. He has never written a single book, so you can imagine how much he knows.

Algernon: I must see him at once on a most important christening – I mean on most important business.

Cecily: Oh!

Algernon: I shan't be away more than half an hour.

Cecily: Considering that we have been engaged since February the 14th, and that I only met you today for the first time, I think it is rather hard that you should leave me for so long a period as half an hour. Couldn't you make it twenty minutes?

Algernon: I'll be back in no time.

[*Kisses her and rushes down the garden.*]

Cecily: What an impetuous boy he is! I like his hair so much. I must enter his proposal in my diary.

> **36** *Bankruptcy Court:* Konkursgericht **57** *impetuous* [ɪm'petʃuəs]: spontaneous; acting without thinking

[*Enter* Merriman.]

Merriman: A Miss Fairfax has just called to see Mr Worthing. On very important business, Miss Fairfax states.

Cecily: Isn't Mr Worthing in his library?

Merriman: Mr Worthing went over in the direction of the Rectory some time ago.

Cecily: Pray ask the lady to come out here; Mr Worthing is sure to be back soon. And you can bring tea.

Merriman: Yes, Miss. [*Goes out.*]

Cecily: Miss Fairfax! I suppose one of the many good elderly women who are associated with Uncle Jack in some of his philanthropic work in London. I don't quite like women who are interested in philanthropic work. I think it is so forward of them.

[*Enter* Merriman.]

Merriman: Miss Fairfax.

[*Enter* Gwendolen. *Exit* Merriman.]

Cecily: [*Advancing to meet her.*] Pray let me introduce myself to you. My name is Cecily Cardew.

Gwendolen: Cecily Cardew? [*Moving to her and shaking hands.*] What a very sweet name! Something tells me that we are going to be great friends. I like you already more than I can say. My first impressions of people are never wrong.

Cecily: How nice of you to like me so much after we have known each other such a comparatively short time. Pray sit down.

Gwendolen: [*Still standing up.*] I may call you Cecily, may I not?

Cecily: With pleasure!

Gwendolen: And you will always call me Gwendolen, won't you?

Cecily: If you wish.

GWENDOLEN: Then that is all quite settled, is it not?

CECILY: I hope so. [*A pause. They both sit down together.*]

GWENDOLEN: Perhaps this might be a favourable opportunity for my mentioning who I am. My father is Lord Bracknell. You have never heard of papa, I suppose?

CECILY: I don't think so.

GWENDOLEN: Outside the family circle, papa, I am glad to say, is entirely unknown. I think that is quite as it should be. The home seems to me to be the proper sphere for the man. And certainly once a man begins to neglect his domestic duties he becomes painfully effeminate, does he not? And I don't like that. It makes men so very attractive. Cecily, mamma, whose views on education are remarkably strict, has brought me up to be extremely short-sighted; it is part of her system; so do you mind my looking at you through my glasses?

CECILY: Oh! not at all, Gwendolen. I am very fond of being looked at.

GWENDOLEN: [*After examining* CECILY *carefully through a lorgnette.*] You are here on a short visit, I suppose.

CECILY: Oh no! I live here.

GWENDOLEN: [*Severely.*] Really? Your mother, no doubt, or some female relative of advanced years, resides here also?

CECILY: Oh no! I have no mother, nor, in fact, any relations.

GWENDOLEN: Indeed?

CECILY: My dear guardian, with the assistance of Miss Prism, has the arduous task of looking after me.

GWENDOLEN: Your guardian?

CECILY: Yes, I am Mr Worthing's ward.

▷ **5** *Rectory:* house where a rector lives **13** *forward* (adj): (here) shameless, immodest **39** *effeminate* [ɪ'femɪnət]: womanly **46** *lorgnette* [lɔːn'jet]: a pair of glasses with a long handle **53** *arduous* ['ɑːdjuəs]: difficult

GWENDOLEN: Oh! It is strange he never mentioned to me that he had a ward. How secretive of him! He grows more interesting hourly. I am not sure, however, that the news inspires me with feelings of unmixed delight. [*Rising and going to her.*] I am very fond of you, Cecily; I have liked you ever since I met you! But I am bound to state that now that I know that you are Mr Worthing's ward, I cannot help expressing a wish you were – well, just a little older than you seem to be – and not quite so very alluring in appearance. In fact, if I may speak candidly –

CECILY: Pray do! I think that whenever one has anything unpleasant to say, one should always be quite candid.

GWENDOLEN: Well, to speak with perfect candour, Cecily, I wish that you were fully forty-two, and more than usually plain for your age. Ernest has a strong upright nature. He is the very soul of truth and honour. Disloyalty would be as impossible to him as deception. But even men of the noblest possible moral character are extremely susceptible to the influence of the physical charms of others. Modern, no less than Ancient History, supplies us with many most painful examples of what I refer to. If it were not so, indeed, History would be quite unreadable.

CECILY: I beg your pardon, Gwendolen, did you say Ernest?

GWENDOLEN: Yes.

CECILY: Oh, but it is not Mr Ernest Worthing who is my guardian. It is his brother – his elder brother.

GWENDOLEN: [*Sitting down again.*] Ernest never mentioned to me that he had a brother.

CECILY: I am sorry to say they have not been on good terms for a long time.

GWENDOLEN: Ah! that accounts for it. And now that I think of it I have never heard any man mention his brother. The subject seems distasteful to most men. Cecily, you have lifted a load from my mind. I was growing almost anxious. It would have been terrible if any cloud had come across a friendship like ours, would it not? Of course you are quite, quite sure that it is not Mr Ernest Worthing who is your guardian?

CECILY: Quite sure. [*A pause.*] In fact, I am going to be his.

GWENDOLEN: [*Enquiringly.*] I beg your pardon?

CECILY: [*Rather shy and confidingly.*] Dearest Gwendolen, there is no reason why I should make a secret of it to you. Our little county newspaper is sure to chronicle the fact next week. Mr Ernest Worthing and I are engaged to be married.

GWENDOLEN: [*Quite politely, rising.*] My darling Cecily, I think there must be some slight error. Mr Ernest Worthing is engaged to me. The announcement will appear in the *Morning Post* on Saturday at the latest.

CECILY: [*Very politely, rising.*] I am afraid you must be under some misconception. Ernest proposed to me exactly ten minutes ago. [*Shows diary.*]

GWENDOLEN: [*Examines diary through her lorgnettte carefully.*] It is very curious, for he asked me to be his wife yesterday afternoon at 5.30. If you would care to verify the incident, pray do so. [*Produces diary of her own.*] I never travel without my diary. One should always have something sensational to read in the train. I am so sorry, dear Cecily, if it is any disappointment to you, but I am afraid *I* have the prior claim.

CECILY: It would distress me more than I can tell you, dear Gwendolen, if it caused you any mental or physical anguish, but I feel bound to point out that since Ernest proposed to you he clearly has changed his mind.

▷ **8** *alluring* [əˈlʊərɪŋ]: attractive **11** *candid:* saying what you think openly and honestly **12** *candour* [ˈkændə]: honesty **15** *disloyalty:* act of being unfaithful • *deception:* act of telling lies or cheating **17** *susceptible:* easily influenced **27** *be on good terms:* have a good relationship **47** *misconception:* misunderstanding **51** *verify sth.:* check that sth. is true **55** *prior claim:* älterer Anspruch **57** *anguish* (n): suffering

Gwendolen: [*Meditatively.*] If the poor fellow has been entrapped into any foolish promise I shall consider it my duty to rescue him at once, and with a firm hand.

Cecily: [*Thoughtfully and sadly.*] Whatever unfortunate entanglement my dear boy may have got into, I will never reproach him with it after we are married.

Gwendolen: Do you allude to me, Miss Cardew, as an entanglement? You are presumptuous. On an occasion of this kind it becomes more than a moral duty to speak one's mind. It becomes a pleasure.

Cecily: Do you suggest, Miss Fairfax, that I entrapped Ernest into an engagement? How dare you? This is no time for wearing the shallow mask of manners. When I see a spade I call it a spade.

Gwendolen: [*Satirically.*] I am glad to say that I have never seen a spade. It is obvious that our social spheres have been widely different.

[*Enter* Merriman, *followed by the footman. He carries a salver, table cloth, and plate stand. Cecily is about to retort. The presence of the servants exercises a restraining influence, under which both girls chafe.*]

Merriman: Shall I lay tea here as usual, Miss?

Cecily: [*Sternly, in a calm voice.*] Yes, as usual.

[Merriman *begins to clear table and lay cloth. A long pause.* Cecily *and* Gwendolen *glare at each other.*]

Gwendolen: Are there many interesting walks in the vicinity, Miss Cardew?

Cecily: Oh! yes! a great many. From the top of one of the hills quite close one can see five counties.

Gwendolen: Five counties! I don't think I should like that; I hate crowds.

Cecily: [*Sweetly.*] I suppose that is why you live in town?

[GWENDOLEN *bites her lip, and beats her foot nervously with her parasol.*]

GWENDOLEN: [*Looking round.*] Quite a well-kept garden this is, Miss Cardew.

CECILY: So glad you like it, Miss Fairfax.

GWENDOLEN: I had no idea there were any flowers in the country.

CECILY: Oh, flowers are as common here, Miss Fairfax, as people are in London.

GWENDOLEN: Personally I cannot understand how anybody manages to exist in the country, if anybody who is anybody does. The country always bores me to death.

CECILY: Ah! This is what the newspapers call agricultural depression, is it not? I believe the aristocracy are suffering very much from it just at present. It is almost an epidemic amongst them, I have been told. May I offer you some tea, Miss Fairfax?

GWENDOLEN: [*With elaborate politeness.*] Thank you. [*Aside.*] Detestable girl! But I require tea!

CECILY: [*Sweetly.*] Sugar?

GWENDOLEN: [*Superciliously.*] No, thank you. Sugar is not fashionable any more.

[CECILY *looks angrily at her, takes up the tongs and puts four lumps of sugar into the cup.*]

▷ **1** *entrapped:* (here) tricked **4–5** *entanglement:* (here) complicated or undesired relationship **5–6** *reproach sb. with sth.:* blame sb. for sth. **8** *presumptuous* [prɪˈzʌmptʃuəs]: arrogant, too confident **13** *call a spade a spade:* speak honestly and clearly **17** *footman:* manservant **18** *plate stand:* stand with three plates on which cakes, etc. are served • *retort* (v): reply quickly to sth. you disagree with **19** *exercise a restraining influence:* (here) force two people to act politely towards each other **20** *chafe:* become annoyed **22** *stern:* serious and disappointing **25** *vicinity:* neighbourhood **33** *parasol:* sunshade **47** *elaborate:* (here) exaggerated **50** *supercilious* [ˌsuːpəˈsɪliəs]: behaving as if you are better than other people

CECILY: [*Severely.*] Cake or bread and butter?

GWENDOLEN: [*In a bored manner.*] Bread and butter, please. Cake is rarely seen at the best houses nowadays.

CECILY: [*Cuts a very large slice of cake and puts it on the tray.*] Hand that to Miss Fairfax.

[MERRIMAN *does so, and goes out with footman.* GWENDOLEN *drinks the tea and makes a grimace. Puts down cup at once, reaches out her hand to the bread and butter, looks at it, and finds it is cake. Rises in indignation.*]

GWENDOLEN: You have filled my tea with lumps of sugar, and though I asked most distinctly for bread and butter, you have given me cake. I am known for the gentleness of my disposition, and the extraordinary sweetness of my nature, but I warn you, Miss Cardew, you may go too far.

CECILY: [*Rising.*] To save my poor, innocent, trusting boy from the machinations of any other girl there are no lengths to which I would not go.

GWENDOLEN: From the moment I saw you I distrusted you. I felt that you were false and deceitful. I am never deceived in such matters. My first impressions of people are invariably right.

CECILY: It seems to me, Miss Fairfax, that I am trespassing on your valuable time. No doubt you have many other calls of a similar character to make in the neighbourhood.

[*Enter* JACK.]

GWENDOLEN: [*Catching sight of him.*] Ernest! My own Ernest!

JACK: Gwendolen! Darling! [*Offers to kiss her.*]

GWENDOLEN: [*Drawing back.*] A moment! May I ask if you are engaged to be married to this young lady? [*Points to* CECILY.]

JACK: [*Laughing.*] To dear little Cecily! Of course not! What could have put such an idea into your pretty little head?

GWENDOLEN: Thank you. You may! [*Offers her cheek.*]

CECILY: [*Very sweetly.*] I knew there must be some misunderstanding, Miss Fairfax. The gentleman whose arm is at present round your waist is my guardian, Mr John Worthing.

GWENDOLEN: I beg your pardon?

CECILY: This is Uncle Jack.

GWENDOLEN: [*Receding.*] Jack! Oh!

[*Enter* ALGERNON.]

CECILY: Here is Ernest.

ALGERNON: [*Goes straight over to* CECILY *without noticing anyone else.*] My own love! [*Offers to kiss her.*]

CECILY: [*Drawing back.*] A moment, Ernest! May I ask you – are you engaged to be married to this young lady?

ALGERNON: [*Looking round.*] To what young lady? Good heavens! Gwendolen!

CECILY: Yes! to good heavens, Gwendolen, I mean to Gwendolen.

ALGERNON: [*Laughing.*] Of course not! What could have put such an idea into your pretty little head?

CECILY: Thank you. [*Presenting her cheek to be kissed.*] You may.

[ALGERNON *kisses her.*]

GWENDOLEN: I felt there was some slight error, Miss Cardew. The gentleman who is now embracing you is my cousin, Mr Algernon Moncrieff.

CECILY: [*Breaking away from* ALGERNON.] Algernon Moncrieff! Oh!

[*The two girls move towards each other and put their arms round each other's waists as if for protection.*]

▷ **16** *machinations:* evil plans • *lengths:* (here) limits, extremes **21** *trespass on sth.* ['--]: (here) waste sth. (esp. time) **37** *recede* [rɪ'siːd]: step backwards

CECILY: Are you called Algernon?

ALGERNON: I cannot deny it.

CECILY: Oh!

GWENDOLEN: Is your name really John?

JACK: [*Standing rather proudly.*] I could deny it if I liked. I could deny anything if I liked. But my name certainly is John. It has been John for years.

CECILY: [*To* GWENDOLEN.] A gross deception has been practised on both of us.

GWENDOLEN: My poor wounded Cecily!

CECILY: My sweet wronged Gwendolen!

GWENDOLEN: [*Slowly and seriously.*] You will call me sister, will you not?

[*They embrace.* JACK *and* ALGERNON *groan and walk up and down.*]

CECILY: [*Rather brightly.*] There is just one question I would like to be allowed to ask my guardian.

GWENDOLEN: An admirable idea! Mr Worthing, there is just one question I would like to be permitted to put to you. Where is your brother Ernest? We are both engaged to be married to your brother Ernest, so it is a matter of some importance to us to know where your brother Ernest is at present.

JACK: [*Slowly and hesitatingly.*] Gwendolen – Cecily – it is very painful for me to be forced to speak the truth. It is the first time in my life that I have ever been reduced to such a painful position, and I am really quite inexperienced in doing anything of the kind. However, I will tell you quite frankly that I have no brother Ernest. I have no brother at all. I never had a brother in my life, and I certainly have not the smallest intention of ever having one in the future.

CECILY: [*Surprised.*] No brother at all?

JACK: [*Cheerily.*] None!

GWENDOLEN: [*Severely.*] Had you never a brother of any kind?

JACK: [*Pleasantly.*] Never. Not even of any kind.

GWENDOLEN: I am afraid it is quite clear, Cecily, that neither of us is engaged to be married to anyone.

CECILY: It is not a very pleasant position for a young girl suddenly to find herself in. Is it?

GWENDOLEN: Let us go into the house. They will hardly venture to come after us there.

CECILY: No, men are so cowardly, aren't they?

[*They retire into the house with scornful looks.*]

JACK: This ghastly state of things is what you call Bunburying, I suppose?

ALGERNON: Yes, and a perfectly wonderful Bunbury it is. The most wonderful Bunbury I have ever had in my life.

JACK: Well, you've no right whatsoever to Bunbury here.

ALGERNON: That is absurd. One has a right to Bunbury anywhere one chooses. Every serious Bunburyist knows that.

JACK: Serious Bunburyist! Good heavens!

ALGERNON: Well, one must be serious about something, if one wants to have any amusement in life. I happen to be serious about Bunburying. What on earth you are serious about I haven't got the remotest idea. About everything, I should fancy. You have such an absolutely trivial nature.

JACK: Well, the only small satisfaction I have in the whole of this wretched business is that your friend Bunbury is quite exploded.

▷ **8–9** *a gross deception has been practised on … us:* a terrible lie has been told to … us **24** *reduced to sth.:* (here) forced into sth. **38** *venture* (v): (here) dare to go somewhere (dangerous) **41** *scornful:* verächtlich **56** *wretched business* ['retʃɪd]: scheußliche Geschichte

You won't be able to run down to the country quite so often as you used to do, dear Algy. And a very good thing too.

ALGERNON: Your brother is a little off colour, isn't he, dear Jack? You won't be able to disappear to London quite so frequently as your wicked custom was. And not a bad thing either.

JACK: As for your conduct towards Miss Cardew, I must say that your taking in a sweet, simple, innocent girl like that is quite inexcusable. To say nothing of the fact that she is my ward.

ALGERNON: I can see no possible defence at all for your deceiving a brilliant, clever, thoroughly experienced young lady like Miss Fairfax. To say nothing of the fact that she is my cousin.

JACK: I wanted to be engaged to Gwendolen, that is all. I love her.

ALGERNON: Well, I simply wanted to be engaged to Cecily. I adore her.

JACK: There is certainly no chance of your marrying Miss Cardew.

ALGERNON: I don't think there is much likelihood, Jack, of you and Miss Fairfax being united.

JACK: Well, that is no business of yours.

ALGERNON: If it was my business, I wouldn't talk about it. [*Begins to eat muffins.*] It is very vulgar to talk about one's business. Only people like stockbrokers do that, and then merely at dinner parties.

JACK: How can you sit there, calmly eating muffins when we are in this horrible trouble, I can't make out. You seem to me to be perfectly heartless.

ALGERNON: Well, I can't eat muffins in an agitated manner. The butter would probably get on my cuffs. One should always eat muffins quite calmly. It is the only way to eat them.

JACK: I say it's perfectly heartless your eating muffins at all, under the circumstances.

ALGERNON: When I am in trouble, eating is the only thing that consoles me. Indeed, when I am in really great trouble, as anyone who knows me intimately will tell you, I refuse everything except food and drink. At the present moment I am eating muffins because I am unhappy. Besides, I am particularly fond of muffins. [*Rising.*]

JACK: [*Rising.*] Well, there is no reason why you should eat them all in that greedy way. [*Takes muffins from* ALGERNON.]

ALGERNON: [*Offering tea-cake.*] I wish you would have tea-cake instead. I don't like tea-cake.

JACK: Good heavens! I suppose a man may eat his own muffins in his own garden.

ALGERNON: But you have just said it was perfectly heartless to eat muffins.

JACK: I said it was perfectly heartless of you, under the circumstances. That is a very different thing.

ALGERNON: That may be. But the muffins are the same. [*He seizes the muffin-dish from* JACK.]

JACK: Algy, I wish to goodness you would go.

ALGERNON: You can't possibly ask me to go without having some dinner. It's absurd. I never go without my dinner. No one ever does, except vegetarians and people like that. Besides I have just made arrangements with Dr Chasuble to be christened at a quarter to six under the name of Ernest.

JACK: My dear fellow, the sooner you give up that nonsense the better. I made arrangements this morning with Dr Chasuble to be christened myself at 5.30, and I naturally will take the name of Ernest. Gwendolen would wish it. We can't both be christened Ernest. It's absurd. Besides, I have a perfect right to be christened

▷ **3** *off colour:* pale; looking unwell **19** *muffin* (BE old-use): type of bread roll that is toasted and eaten with butter **20** *stockbroker:* Börsenmakler/in **25** *agitated* (adj): worried, nervous **31** *console sb.:* make sb. feel better .

if I like. There is no evidence at all that I have ever been christened by anybody. I should think it extremely probable I never was, and so does Dr Chasuble. It is entirely different in your case. You have been christened already.

ALGERNON: Yes, but I have not been christened for years.

JACK: Yes, but you have been christened. That is the important thing.

ALGERNON: Quite so. So I know my constitution can stand it. If you are not quite sure about your ever having been christened, I must say I think it rather dangerous your venturing on it now. It might make you very unwell. You can hardly have forgotten that someone very closely connected with you was very nearly carried off this week in Paris by a severe chill.

JACK: Yes, but you said yourself that a severe chill was not hereditary.

ALGERNON: It usen't to be, I know – but I daresay it is now. Science is always making wonderful improvements in things.

JACK: [*Picking up the muffin-dish.*] Oh, that is nonsense; you are always talking nonsense.

ALGERNON: Jack, you are at the muffins again! I wish you wouldn't. There are only two left. [*Takes them.*] I told you I was particularly fond of muffins.

JACK: But I hate tea-cake.

ALGERNON: Why on earth then do you allow tea-cake to be served up for your guests? What ideas you have of hospitality!

JACK: Algernon! I have already told you to go. I don't want you here. Why don't you go!

ALGERNON: I haven't quite finished my tea yet! and there is still one muffin left.

[JACK *groans, and sinks into a chair.* ALGERNON *still continues eating.*]

ACT DROP

THIRD ACT

Scene: Morning-room at the Manor House.
GWENDOLEN *and* CECILY *are at the window, looking out into the garden.*

GWENDOLEN: The fact that they did not follow us at once into the house, as anyone else would have done, seems to me to show that they have some sense of shame left.

CECILY: They have been eating muffins. That looks like repentance.

GWENDOLEN: [*After a pause.*] They don't seem to notice us at all. Couldn't you cough?

CECILY: But I haven't got a cough.

GWENDOLEN: They're looking at us. What effrontery!

CECILY: They're approaching. That's very forward of them.

GWENDOLEN: Let us preserve a dignified silence.

CECILY: Certainly. It's the only thing to do now.

[*Enter* JACK *followed by* ALGERNON. *They whistle some dreadful popular air from a British Opera.*]

GWENDOLEN: This dignified silence seems to produce an unpleasant effect.

CECILY: A most distasteful one.

GWENDOLEN: But we will not be the first to speak.

CECILY: Certainly not.

GWENDOLEN: Mr Worthing, I have something very particular to ask you. Much depends on your reply.

▷ **7** *my constitution can stand it:* (here) I am fit enough to do it **9** *venture on sth.:* (here) risk sth **36** *repentance:* quality of feeling sorry for having done sth. wrong **40** *What effrontery!* [ɪ'frʌntəri]: How shameless! **42** *preserve sth.:* keep sth.

Cecily: Gwendolen, your common sense is invaluable. Mr Moncrieff, kindly answer me the following question. Why did you pretend to be my guardian's brother?

Algernon: In order that I might have an opportunity of meeting you.

Cecily: [*To* Gwendolen.] That certainly seems a satisfactory explanation, does it not?

Gwendolen: Yes, dear, if you can believe him.

Cecily: I don't. But that does not affect the wonderful beauty of his answer.

Gwendolen: True. In matters of grave importance, style, not sincerity, is the vital thing. Mr Worthing, what explanation can you offer to me for pretending to have a brother? Was it in order that you might have an opportunity of coming up to town to see me as often as possible?

Jack: Can you doubt it, Miss Fairfax?

Gwendolen: I have the gravest doubts upon the subject. But I intend to crush them. This is not the moment for German scepticism. [*Moving to* Cecily.] Their explanations appear to be quite satisfactory, especially Mr Worthing's. That seems to me to have the stamp of truth upon it.

Cecily: I am more than content with what Mr Moncrieff said. His voice alone inspires one with absolute credulity.

Gwendolen: Then you think we should forgive them?

Cecily: Yes. I mean no.

Gwendolen: True! I had forgotten. There are principles at stake that one cannot surrender. Which of us should tell them? The task is not a pleasant one.

Cecily: Could we not both speak at the same time?

Gwendolen: An excellent idea! I nearly always speak at the same time as other people. Will you take the time from me?

CECILY: Certainly.

[GWENDOLEN *beats time with uplifted finger.*]

GWENDOLEN and CECILY: [*Speaking together.*] Your Christian names are still an insuperable barrier. That is all!

JACK and ALGERNON: [*Speaking together.*] Our Christian names! Is that all? But we are going to be christened this afternoon.

GWENDOLEN: [*To* JACK.] For my sake you are prepared to do this terrible thing?

JACK: I am.

CECILY: [*To* ALGERNON.] To please me you are ready to face this fearful ordeal?

ALGERNON: I am!

GWENDOLEN: How absurd to talk of the equality of the sexes! Where questions of self-sacrifice are concerned, men are infinitely beyond us.

JACK: We are. [*Clasps hands with* ALGERNON.]

CECILY: They have moments of physical courage of which we women know absolutely nothing.

GWENDOLEN: [*To* JACK.] Darling!

ALGERNON: [*To* CECILY.] Darling! [*They fall into each other's arms.*]

[*Enter* MERRIMAN. *When he enters he coughs loudly, seeing the situation.*]

MERRIMAN: Ahem! Ahem! Lady Bracknell!

▷ **8** *affect sth.:* (here) not change your views of sth. **17** *scepticism:* state of having doubts about morals and beliefs **22** *credulity* [krɪ'dju:ləti] (n): willingness to believe that sth. is true or real **30** *take the time from sb.:* (here) follow the timing and rhythm as signalled by sb. **34** *insuperable* [ɪn'su:pərəbl] (fml): (here) that cannot be overcome **40** *fearful* (fml): (here) frightening **41** *ordeal* [ɔ:'di:l]: terrible or unpleasant experience

Jack: Good heavens!

[*Enter* Lady Bracknell. *The couples separate in alarm. Exit* Merriman.]

Lady Bracknell: Gwendolen! What does this mean?

Gwendolen: Merely that I am engaged to be married to Mr Worthing, mamma.

Lady Bracknell: Come here. Sit down. Sit down immediately. Hesitation of any kind is a sign of mental decay in the young, of physical weakness in the old. [*Turns to* Jack.] Apprised, sir, of my daughter's sudden flight by her trusty maid, whose confidence I purchased by means of a small coin, I followed her at once by a luggage train. Her unhappy father is, I am glad to say, under the impression that she is attending a more than usually lengthy lecture by the University Extension Scheme on the Influence of a permanent income on Thought. I do not propose to undeceive him. Indeed I have never undeceived him on any question. I would consider it wrong. But of course, you will clearly understand that all communication between yourself and my daughter must cease immediately from this moment. On this point, as indeed on all points, I am firm.

Jack: I am engaged to be married to Gwendolen, Lady Bracknell!

Lady Bracknell: You are nothing of the kind, sir. And now, as regards Algernon! ... Algernon!

Algernon: Yes, Aunt Augusta.

Lady Bracknell: May I ask if it is in this house that your invalid friend Mr Bunbury resides?

Algernon: [*Stammering.*] Oh! No! Bunbury doesn't live here. Bunbury is somewhere else at present. In fact, Bunbury is dead.

Lady Bracknell: Dead! When did Mr Bunbury die? His death must have been extremely sudden.

ALGERNON: [*Airily.*] Oh! I killed Bunbury this afternoon. I mean poor Bunbury died this afternoon.

LADY BRACKNELL: What did he die of?

ALGERNON: Bunbury? Oh, he was quite exploded.

LADY BRACKNELL: Exploded! Was he the victim of a revolutionary outrage? I was not aware that Mr Bunbury was interested in social legislation. If so, he is well punished for his morbidity.

ALGERNON: My dear Aunt Augusta, I mean he was found out! The doctors found out that Bunbury could not live, that is what I mean – so Bunbury died.

LADY BRACKNELL: He seems to have had great confidence in the opinion of his physicians. I am glad, however, that he made up his mind at the last to some definite course of action, and acted under proper medical advice. And now that we have finally got rid of this Mr Bunbury, may I ask, Mr Worthing, who is that young person whose hand my nephew Algernon is now holding in what seems to me a peculiarly unnecessary manner?

JACK: That lady is Miss Cecily Cardew, my ward.

[LADY BRACKNELL *bows coldly to* CECILY.]

ALGERNON: I am engaged to be married to Cecily, Aunt Augusta.

LADY BRACKNELL: I beg your pardon?

CECILY: Mr Moncrieff and I are engaged to be married, Lady Bracknell.

LADY BRACKNELL: [*With a shiver, crossing to the sofa and sitting down.*] I do not know whether there is anything peculiarly

▷ **9** *apprise sb. of sth.* [ə'praɪz] (v; fml): inform sb. of sth. **10** *trusty* (adj) (fml): faithful, trustworthy **11** *purchase sth.* ['pɜːtʃəs]: buy sth. **12** *luggage train:* train that transports only goods, etc. **14** *University Extension Scheme:* University teaching programme for the general public **16** *undeceive sb.:* (here) tell sb. the truth **37** *legislation:* Gesetzgebung • *morbidity:* strong interest in unpleasant matters **42–43** *make up your mind:* decide **43** *at the last:* (here) in the end, finally **54** *shiver* (n): Schauder

exciting in the air of this particular part of Hertfordshire, but the number of engagements that go on seems to me considerably above the proper average that statistics have laid down for our guidance. I think some preliminary enquiry on my part would not be out of place. Mr Worthing, is Miss Cardew at all connected with any of the larger railway stations in London? I merely desire information. Until yesterday I had no idea that there were any families or persons whose origin was a Terminus.

[JACK *looks perfectly furious, but restrains himself.*]

JACK: [*In a clear, cold voice.*] Miss Cardew is the granddaughter of the late Mr Thomas Cardew of 149 Belgrave Square, S.W.; Gervase Park, Dorking, Surrey; and the Sporran, Fifeshire, N.B.

LADY BRACKNELL: That sounds not unsatisfactory. Three addresses always inspire confidence, even in tradesmen. But what proof have I of their authenticity?

JACK: I have carefully preserved the Court Guides of the period. They are open to your inspection, Lady Bracknell.

LADY BRACKNELL: [*Grimly.*] I have known strange errors in that publication.

JACK: Miss Cardew's family solicitors are Messrs Markby, Markby, and Markby.

LADY BRACKNELL: Markby, Markby, and Markby? A firm of the very highest position in their profession. Indeed I am told that one of the Mr Markbys is occasionally to be seen at dinner parties. So far I am satisfied.

JACK: [*Very irritably.*] How extremely kind of you, Lady Bracknell! I have also in my possession, you will be pleased to hear, certificates of Miss Cardew's birth, baptism, whooping cough, registration, vaccination, confirmation, and the measles; both the German and the English variety.

LADY BRACKNELL: Ah! A life crowded with incident, I see; though perhaps somewhat too exciting for a young girl. I am not myself in favour of premature experiences. [*Rises, looks at her watch.*] Gwendolen! the time approaches for our departure. We have not a moment to lose. As a matter of form, Mr Worthing, I had better ask you if Miss Cardew has any little fortune?

JACK: Oh! about a hundred and thirty thousand pounds in the Funds. That is all. Goodbye, Lady Bracknell. So pleased to have seen you.

LADY BRACKNELL: [*Sitting down again.*] A moment, Mr Worthing. A hundred and thirty thousand pounds! And in the Funds! Miss Cardew seems to me a most attractive young lady, now that I look at her. Few girls of the present day have any really solid qualities, any of the qualities that last, and improve with time. We live, I regret to say, in an age of surfaces. [*To* CECILY.] Come over here, dear. [CECILY *goes across.*] Pretty child! your dress is sadly simple, and your hair seems almost as Nature might have left it. But we can soon alter all that. A thoroughly experienced French maid produces a really marvellous result in a very brief space of time. I remember recommending one to young Lady Lancing, and after three months her own husband did not know her.

JACK: And after six months nobody knew her.

LADY BRACKNELL: [*Glares at* JACK *for a few moments. Then bends, with a practised smile, to* CECILY.] Kindly turn round, sweet child. [CECILY *turns completely round.*] No, the side view is what I want. [CECILY *presents her profile.*] Yes, quite as I expected. There are distinct social possibilities in your profile. The two weak points in our age are its want of principle and its want of profile. The chin a

▷ **4** *enquiry* (n): act of asking questions in order to collect information • *on my part:* by me **8** *Terminus:* (here) station at the end of a railway line **12** *the Sporran:* leather pouch or bag worn over a kilt • *Fifeshire* (usu. *Fife*): county in Scotland • *N.B.* (abbr) = *North Britain:* (old-use) Scotland **16** *Court Guides:* annual publications with names and addresses of members of the British aristocracy **20** *solicitor* [sə'lɪsɪtə]: Rechtsanwalt/-wältin • *Messrs* ['mesəz] (fml): plural of Mr. used before a list of names **28** *whooping cough* ['hu:pɪŋ kɒf]: Keuchhusten **29** *vaccination:* Impfung • *measles* ['mi:zlz]: Masern **30** *German measles:* Röteln **31** *crowded with:* (here) full of **37** *the Funds:* governments stocks (= Staatsanleihe), which gave a good income with very little risk **53** *practised:* (here) well trained; artificial **57** *want of sth.:* not having sth., being without sth.

little higher, dear. Style largely depends on the way the chin is worn. They are worn very high, just at present, Algernon!

ALGERNON: Yes, Aunt Augusta!

LADY BRACKNELL: There are distinct social possibilities in Miss Cardew's profile.

ALGERNON: Cecily is the sweetest, dearest, prettiest girl in the whole world. And I don't care twopence about social possibilities.

LADY BRACKNELL: Never speak disrespectfully of Society, Algernon. Only people who can't get into it do that. [*To* CECILY.] Dear child, of course you know that Algernon has nothing but his debts to depend upon. But I do not approve of mercenary marriages. When I married Lord Bracknell I had no fortune of any kind. But I never dreamed for a moment of allowing that to stand in my way. Well, I suppose I must give my consent.

ALGERNON: Thank you, Aunt Augusta.

LADY BRACKNELL: Cecily, you may kiss me!

CECILY: [*Kisses her.*] Thank you, Lady Bracknell.

LADY BRACKNELL: You may also address me as Aunt Augusta for the future.

CECILY: Thank you, Aunt Augusta.

LADY BRACKNELL: The marriage, I think, had better take place quite soon.

ALGERNON: Thank you, Aunt Augusta.

CECILY: Thank you, Aunt Augusta.

LADY BRACKNELL: To speak frankly, I am not in favour of long engagements. They give people the opportunity of finding out each other's character before marriage, which I think is never advisable.

JACK: I beg your pardon for interrupting you, Lady Bracknell, but this engagement is quite out of the question. I am Miss Cardew's guardian, and she cannot marry without my consent until she comes of age. That consent I absolutely decline to give.

LADY BRACKNELL: Upon what grounds may I ask? Algernon is an extremely, I may almost say an ostentatiously, eligible young man. He has nothing, but he looks everything. What more can one desire?

JACK: It pains me very much to have to speak frankly to you, Lady Bracknell, about your nephew, but the fact is that I do not approve at all of his moral character. I suspect him of being untruthful.

[ALGERNON *and* CECILY *look at him in indignant amazement.*]

LADY BRACKNELL: Untruthful! My nephew Algernon? Impossible! He is an Oxonian.

JACK: I fear there can be no possible doubt about the matter. This afternoon during my temporary absence in London on an important question of romance, he obtained admission to my house by means of the false pretence of being my brother. Under an assumed name he drank, I've just been informed by my butler, an entire pint bottle of my Perrier-Jouet, Brut, '89; wine I was specially reserving for myself. Continuing his disgraceful deception, he succeeded in the course of the afternoon in alienating the affections of my only ward. He subsequently stayed to tea, and devoured every single muffin. And what makes his conduct all the more heartless is, that he was perfectly well aware from the first that I have no brother, that I never had a brother, and that I don't intend to have a brother, not even of any kind. I distinctly told him so myself yesterday afternoon.

LADY BRACKNELL: Ahem! Mr Worthing, after careful consideration I have decided entirely to overlook my nephew's conduct to you.

▷ **11** *mercenary* ['mɜːsənəri]: geldgewinnend **31** *come of age:* volljährig werden • *decline* (v): (here) refuse **33** *ostentatiously:* (here) extremely; in a way that is very obvious • *eligible young man:* person who would be a good choice as a husband **41** *Oxonian* [ɒk'səʊniən]: person who studied at Oxford University **44** *obtain admission to sth.:* (here) enter sth. **46** *assumed:* (here) false **49** *alienate sth.* ['eɪliəneɪt]: (hier) etwas entfremden **50** *subsequently:* (here) afterwards, later

Jack: That is very generous of you, Lady Bracknell. My own decision, however, is unalterable. I decline to give my consent.

Lady Bracknell: [*To* Cecily.] Come here, sweet child. [Cecily *goes over.*] How old are you, dear?

Cecily: Well, I am really only eighteen, but I always admit to twenty when I go to evening parties.

Lady Bracknell: You are perfectly right in making some slight alteration. Indeed, no woman should ever be quite accurate about her age. It looks so calculating ... [*In a meditative manner.*] Eighteen, but admitting to twenty at evening parties. Well, it will not be very long before you are of age and free from the restraints of tutelage. So I don't think your guardian's consent is, after all, a matter of any importance.

Jack: Pray excuse me, Lady Bracknell, for interrupting you again, but it is only fair to tell you that according to the terms of her grandfather's will Miss Cardew does not come legally of age till she is thirty-five.

Lady Bracknell: That does not seem to me to be a grave objection. Thirty-five is a very attractive age. London society is full of women of the very highest birth who have, of their own free choice, remained thirty-five for years. Lady Dumbleton is an instance in point. To my own knowledge she has been thirty-five ever since she arrived at the age of forty, which was many years ago now. I see no reason why our dear Cecily should not be even still more attractive at the age you mention than she is at present. There will be a large accumulation of property.

Cecily: Algy, could you wait for me till I was thirty-five?

Algernon: Of course I could, Cecily. You know I could.

Cecily: Yes, I felt it instinctively, but I couldn't wait all that time. I hate waiting even five minutes for anybody. It always makes me rather cross. I am not punctual myself, I know, but I do like punctuality in others, and waiting, even to be married, is quite out of the question.

ALGERNON: Then what is to be done, Cecily?

CECILY: I don't know, Mr Moncrieff.

LADY BRACKNELL: My dear Mr Worthing, as Miss Cardew states positively that she cannot wait till she is thirty-five – a remark which I am bound to say seems to me to show a somewhat impatient nature – I would beg of you to reconsider your decision.

JACK: But my dear Lady Bracknell, the matter is entirely in your own hands. The moment you consent to my marriage with Gwendolen, I will most gladly allow your nephew to form an alliance with my ward.

LADY BRACKNELL: [*Rising and drawing herself up.*] You must be quite aware that what you propose is out of the question.

JACK: Then a passionate celibacy is all that any of us can look forward to.

LADY BRACKNELL: That is not the destiny I propose for Gwendolen. Algernon, of course, can choose for himself. [*Pulls out her watch.*] Come, dear, [GWENDOLEN *rises.*] we have already missed five, if not six, trains. To miss any more might expose us to comment on the platform.

[*Enter* DR CHASUBLE.]

CHASUBLE: Everything is quite ready for the christenings.

LADY BRACKNELL: The christenings, sir! Is not that somewhat premature?

CHASUBLE: [*Looking rather puzzled, and pointing to* JACK *and* ALGERNON.] Both these gentlemen have expressed a desire for immediate baptism.

LADY BRACKNELL: At their age? The idea is grotesque and irreligious! Algernon, I forbid you to be baptized. I will not hear of such

▷ **2** *unalterable:* that cannot be changed **11–12** *restraints of tutelage:* Ketten der Vormundschaft **21–22** *instance in point:* (here) perfect example **37** *positively:* (here) clearly and firmly **44** *draw yourself up:* sich aufrichten

excesses. Lord Bracknell would be highly displeased if he learned that that was the way in which you wasted your time and money.

Chasuble: Am I to understand then that there are to be no christenings at all this afternoon?

Jack: I don't think that, as things are now, it would be of much practical value to either of us, Dr Chasuble.

Chasuble: I am grieved to hear such sentiments from you, Mr Worthing. They savour of the heretical views of the Anabaptists, views that I have completely refuted in four of my unpublished sermons. However, as your present mood seems to be one peculiarly secular, I will return to the church at once. Indeed, I have just been informed by the pew-opener that for the last hour and a half Miss Prism has been waiting for me in the vestry.

Lady Bracknell: [*Starting.*] Miss Prism! Did I hear you mention a Miss Prism?

Chasuble: Yes, Lady Bracknell. I am on my way to join her.

Lady Bracknell: Pray allow me to detain you for a moment. This matter may prove to be one of vital importance to Lord Bracknell and myself. Is this Miss Prism a female of repellent aspect, remotely connected with education?

Chasuble: [*Somewhat indignantly.*] She is the most cultivated of ladies, and the very picture of respectability.

Lady Bracknell: It is obviously the same person. May I ask what position she holds in your household?

Chasuble: [*Severely.*] I am a celibate, madam.

Jack: [*Interposing.*] Miss Prism, Lady Bracknell, has been for the last three years Miss Cardew's esteemed governess and valued companion.

Lady Bracknell: In spite of what I hear of her, I must see her at once. Let her be sent for.

Chasuble: [*Looking off.*] She approaches; she is nigh.

[*Enter* Miss Prism *hurriedly*.]

Miss Prism: I was told you expected me in the vestry, dear Canon. I have been waiting for you there for an hour and three-quarters. [*Catches sight of* Lady Bracknell, *who has fixed her with a stony glare.* Miss Prism *grows pale and quails. She looks anxiously round as if desirous to escape.*]

Lady Bracknell: [*In a severe, judicial voice.*] Prism! [Miss Prism *bows her head in shame.*] Come here, Prism! [Miss Prism *approaches in a humble manner.*] Prism! Where is that baby? [*General consternation. The Canon starts back in horror.* Algernon *and* Jack *pretend to be anxious to shield* Cecily *and* Gwendolen *from hearing the details of a terrible public scandal.*] Twenty-eight years ago, Prism, you left Lord Bracknell's house, Number 104, Upper Grosvenor Street, in charge of a perambulator that contained a baby, of the male sex. You never returned. A few weeks later, through the elaborate investigations of the Metropolitan police, the perambulator was discovered at midnight, standing by itself in a remote corner of Bayswater. It contained the manuscript of a three-volume novel of more than usually revolting sentimentality. [Miss Prism *starts in involuntary indignation.*] But the baby was not there. [*Everyone looks at* Miss Prism.] Prism! Where is that baby?

Miss Prism: [*After a pause.*] Lady Bracknell, I admit with shame that I do not know. I only wish I did. The plain facts of the case are

▷ **8** *savour of sth.* ['seɪvə]: (here) sound like sth. (bad) • *heretical views:* ketzerische Überzeugungen • *Anabaptists:* Christian sect that does not believe in the baptism of children **9** *refute sth.:* prove sth. to be wrong **11** *secular* ['sekjələ]: non-religious, worldly **12** pew-opener: person who unlocks the doors of the individual pews (= Kirchenbänke) **13** *vestry:* Sakristei **14** *start* (v): (hier) aufschrecken, auffahren **17** *detain sb.* (fml): (here) delay sb. **18** *vital* ['vaɪtl]: (here) great, essential **19** *repellent* (fml): very unpleasant • *aspect:* appearance, looks **26** *interpose:* (here) interrupt **31** *nigh* [naɪ] (fml): near **36** *quail* [kweɪl] (v; fml): shake with fear **41** *consternation:* alarm, shock **46** *perambulator* [pə'ræmbjuleɪtə] (old-use): four-wheeled carriage in which babies can be pushed **47** *elaborate* [ɪ'læbəreɪt] (adj): (here) careful and done in great detail **49** *remote:* (here) far, distant, isolated **51** *revolting* (adj): (here) extremely unpleasant **51–52** *in involuntary indignation:* in unwillkürlicher Entrüstung

these. On the morning of the day you mention, a day that is for ever branded on my memory, I prepared as usual to take the baby out in its perambulator. I had also with me a somewhat old, but capacious hand-bag in which I had intended to place the manuscript of a work of fiction that I had written during my few unoccupied hours. In a moment of mental abstraction, for which I never can forgive myself, I deposited the manuscript in the bassinette, and placed the baby in the hand-bag.

JACK: [*Who has been listening attentively.*] But where did you deposit the hand-bag?

MISS PRISM: Do not ask me, Mr Worthing.

JACK: Miss Prism, this is a matter of no small importance to me. I insist on knowing where you deposited the hand-bag that contained that infant.

MISS PRISM: I left it in the cloak-room of one of the larger railway stations in London.

JACK: What railway station?

MISS PRISM: [*Quite crushed.*] Victoria. The Brighton line. [*Sinks into a chair.*]

JACK: I must retire to my room for a moment. Gwendolen, wait here for me.

GWENDOLEN: If you are not too long, I will wait here for you all my life.

[*Exit* JACK *in great excitement.*]

CHASUBLE: What do you think this means, Lady Bracknell?

LADY BRACKNELL: I dare not even suspect, Dr Chasuble. I need hardly tell you that in families of high position strange coincidences are not supposed to occur. They are hardly considered the thing.

[*Noises heard overhead as if someone was throwing trunks about. Everyone looks up.*]

Cecily: Uncle Jack seems strangely agitated.

Chasuble: Your guardian has a very emotional nature.

Lady Bracknell: This noise is extremely unpleasant. It sounds as if he was having an argument. I dislike arguments of any kind. They are always vulgar, and often convincing.

Chasuble: [*Looking up.*] It has stopped now.

[*The noise is redoubled.*]

Lady Bracknell: I wish he would arrive at some conclusion.

Gwendolen: This suspense is terrible. I hope it will last.

[*Enter* Jack *with a hand-bag of black leather in his hand.*]

Jack: [*Rushing over to* Miss Prism.] Is this the handbag, Miss Prism? Examine it carefully before you speak. The happiness of more than one life depends on your answer.

Miss Prism: [*Calmly.*] It seems to be mine. Yes, here is the injury it received through the upsetting of a Gower Street omnibus in younger and happier days. Here is the stain on the lining caused by the explosion of a temperance beverage, an incident that occurred at Leamington. And here, on the lock, are my initials. I had forgotten that in an extravagant mood I had had them placed there. The bag is undoubtedly mine. I am delighted to have it so unexpectedly restored to me. It has been a great inconvenience being without it all these years.

Jack: [*In a pathetic voice.*] Miss Prism, more is restored to you than this hand-bag. I was the baby you placed in it.

Miss Prism: [*Amazed.*] You?

▷ **4** *capacious* [kəˈpeɪʃəs](fml): very large, with a lot of room **6** *mental abstraction:* (here) forgetfulness **7** *deposit sth.* [dɪˈpɒzɪt]: put sth., place sth. • *bassinette:* baby-carriage **18** *crushed:* (hier) niedergeschmettert **26** *suspect* [səˈspekt] (v): (here) imagine **28** *be considered the thing:* (here) be respected in society **44** *injury:* (here) damage **45** *upsetting:* (here) accident **46** *lining* (n): Futter **47** *temperance beverage* (fml): non-alcoholic drink **48** *Leamington:* a spa town between London and Birmingham **53** *pathetic:* (here) sentimental

JACK: [*Embracing her.*] Yes – mother!

MISS PRISM: [*Recoiling in indignant astonishment.*] Mr Worthing! I am unmarried!

JACK: Unmarried! I do not deny that is a serious blow. But after all, who has the right to cast a stone against one who has suffered? Cannot repentance wipe out an act of folly? Why should there be one law for men, and another for women? Mother, I forgive you. [*Tries to embrace her again.*]

MISS PRISM: [*Still more indignant.*] Mr Worthing, there is some error. [*Pointing to* LADY BRACKNELL.] There is the lady who can tell you who you really are.

[*A pause.*]

JACK: Lady Bracknell, I hate to seem inquisitive, but would you kindly inform me who I am?

LADY BRACKNELL: I am afraid that the news I have to give you will not altogether please you. You are the son of my poor sister, Mrs. Moncrieff, and consequently Algernon's elder brother.

JACK: Algy's elder brother! Then I have a brother after all. I knew I had a brother! I always said I had a brother! Cecily – how could you have ever doubted that I had a brother? [*Seizes hold of* ALGERNON.] Dr Chasuble, my unfortunate brother. Miss Prism, my unfortunate brother. Gwendolen, my unfortunate brother. Algy, you young scoundrel, you will have to treat me with more respect in the future. You have never behaved to me like a brother in all your life.

ALGERNON: Well, not till today, old boy, I admit. I did my best, however, though I was out of practice.

[*Shakes hands.*]

GWENDOLEN: [*To* JACK.] My own! But what own are you? What is your Christian name, now that you have become someone else?

JACK: Good heavens! – I had quite forgotten that point. Your decision on the subject of my name is irrevocable, I suppose?

GWENDOLEN: I never change, except in my affections.

CECILY: What a noble nature you have, Gwendolen!

JACK: Then the question had better be cleared up at once. Aunt Augusta, a moment. At the time when Miss Prism left me in the hand-bag, had I been christened already?

LADY BRACKNELL: Every luxury that money could buy, including christening, had been lavished on you by your fond and doting parents.

JACK: Then I was christened! That is settled. Now, what name was I given? Let me know the worst.

LADY BRACKNELL: Being the eldest son you were naturally christened after your father.

JACK: [*Irritably.*] Yes, but what was my father's Christian name?

LADY BRACKNELL: [*Meditatively.*] I cannot at the present moment recall what the General's Christian name was. But I have no doubt he had one. He was eccentric, I admit. But only in later years. And that was the result of the Indian climate, and marriage, and indigestion, and other things of that kind.

JACK: Algy! Can't you recollect what our father's Christian name was?

ALGERNON: My dear boy, we were never even on speaking terms. He died before I was a year old.

JACK: His name would appear in the Army Lists of the period, I suppose, Aunt Augusta?

▷ **2** *recoil* (v): (here) step back quickly and in horror **26** *old boy* (infml): (here) alter Junge **32** *irrevocable* [ɪ'revəkəbl] (fml): that cannot be changed **39** *lavish sth. on sb.:* give a lot or too much of sth. to sb. • *fond* (adj): feeling affection for sb. • *doting* ['dəʊtɪŋ] (adj): showing a lot of love for sb. **50** *indigestion* [ˌɪndɪ'dʒestʃən]: Magenschmerzen/-verstimmung **51** *recollect sth.* [ˌrekə'lekt] (fml): remember sth. **54** *Army Lists:* official lists of all officers in the British army

LADY BRACKNELL: The General was essentially a man of peace, except in his domestic life. But I have no doubt his name would appear in any military directory.

JACK: The Army Lists of the last forty years are here. These delightful records should have been my constant study. [*Rushes to bookcase and tears the books out.*] M. Generals ... Mallam, Maxbohm, Magley – what ghastly names they have – Markby, Migsby, Mobbs, Moncrieff! Lieutenant 1840, Captain, Lieutenant-Colonel, Colonel, General 1869, Christian names, Ernest John. [*Puts book very quietly down and speaks quite calmly.*] I always told you, Gwendolen, my name was Ernest, didn't I? Well, it is Ernest after all. I mean it naturally is Ernest.

LADY BRACKNELL: Yes, I remember now that the General was called Ernest. I knew I had some particular reason for disliking the name.

GWENDOLEN: Ernest! My own Ernest! I felt from the first that you could have no other name!

JACK: Gwendolen, it is a terrible thing for a man to find out suddenly that all his life he has been speaking nothing but the truth. Can you forgive me?

GWENDOLEN: I can. For I feel that you are sure to change.

JACK: My own one!

CHASUBLE: [*To* MISS PRISM.] Laetitia! [*Embraces her.*]

MISS PRISM: [*Enthusiastically.*] Frederick! At last!

ALGERNON: Cecily! [*Embraces her.*] At last!

JACK: Gwendolen! [*Embraces her.*] At last!

LADY BRACKNELL: My nephew, you seem to be displaying signs of triviality.

JACK: On the contrary, Aunt Augusta, I've now realized for the first time in my life the vital Importance of Being Earnest.

CURTAIN

THE AUTHOR

© Mary Evans Picture Library/Photograph Ellis & Wallery

Oscar Wilde was born in Dublin, Ireland (then part of the United Kingdom), in 1854. His father was a famous eye surgeon with strong interests in archaeology and Irish oral folklore. His mother was a writer and supporter of women's rights and Irish independence.

Wilde studied at Trinity College Dublin and then Oxford University. On completing his studies he moved to London in 1878. He married Constance Lloyd in 1884 with whom he had two sons.

The period 1888–1895 was Wilde's most productive literary period. He wrote articles and various collections of stories, while becoming the leading member of the Aesthetic Movement, which believed in 'art for art's sake'. In 1891 he published his only novel *The Picture of Dorian Gray*. In 1892 his play *Lady Windermere's Fan* opened in London, which was followed by *A Woman of No Importance* (1893) and *An Ideal Husband* (1894). *The Importance of Being Earnest* opened on 14 February 1895. The Prince of Wales was in the audience and the play was an instant success.

However, in May 1895 Oscar Wilde was found guilty of 'acts of gross indecency with other male persons', i.e. homosexual relations. He was sentenced to two years hard labour. He left prison in 1897 and spent the rest of his life in poverty in France. Wilde's last work, the poem 'The Ballad of Reading Jail', was published anonymously in 1898. He died in a shabby hotel in Paris in 1900.